A Beautiful Pain

The Story of a Violent Juvenile Offender Sentenced to Life in Prison at 16 and His Transformation into a Community Advocate.

Damon D. Venable

SPECIAL NOTE: To all corporations, universities, colleges, higher learning, religious and professional organizations: Quantity discounts are available on bulk purchases of this book for educational, gift purposes or as premiums for increasing magazine subscriptions or renewals. For additional information and book requests, please contact **www.damondvenable.com**

THIS IS A WRITTEN WORK BY
DAMON D. VENABLE
PUBLISHED BY HARVEST WEALTH PUBLISHING LLC

This is a work of non-fiction based on the boyhood memoirs of **Damon D. Venable.**
Some names and identifying details of factual accounts to protect the privacy of individuals who have successfully moved on with their lives and who understandably wish to forget the horrors of their misguided criminal pasts as minors growing up in a violent urban environment in America during the 80s.

A Beautiful Pain

Published in the United States of America by
Harvest Wealth Publishing LLC 2025
An imprint of Harvest Wealth Publishing LLC

www.damondvenable.com

Library of Congress Cataloguing-In-Publication Number
PENDING

ISBN 979-8-9871782-1-8
First Edition Printing
Printed in the United States of America
October 2025

Harvest Wealth Publishing LLC
371 Hoes Lane Suite 200
Piscataway, NJ 08854

Dedication

This book is dedicated to Mrs. Bernadine Gilliam Venable (11/23/1950-6/21/2018), my mother, whose unwavering love and support for me, despite my utter failures and heart-wrenching disappointments, continuously illumines my life. And to my baby sister, Trunetta Woody (01/06/1982-09/23/2025), who was so proud of her big brother and never failed to let me and the world know it; and also to every family who has experienced the violent victimization of the state-sanctioned, racialized mass incarceration project because they were Otherized.

Damon's Acknowledgments

To my father, Marvin Emmet Venable, Sr. (3/17/1945-8/29/2017), one of the greatest men I've met and who wanted simply to -"live an enjoyable life and then live on through my children." I say, "Thank you for the invaluable life lessons Dad, you're with me always!"

So as not to exclude anyone, I want to thank every amazing human being I encountered in my life who exemplified why I must not bargain with the voice of mediocrity. Because of you all, I am no longer imprisoned by a self-defeating, self-hating, and uneducated mindset—A mindset that caused me to become a violent juvenile offender in my own community and imprisoned me even before I was sent to prison.

I want to acknowledge all the men and women still behind bars, imprisoned to death-in-life sentences for just being young, traumatized, non-white, and/or poor that - "I am committed to disproving the myth that we are irredeemable!"

I want to thank all my siblings, extended family, system-impacted community, and dear, dear friends (you all know who you are) for your ceaseless encouragement and support over the decades and/or for showing me what freedom feels like since my release.

This book would not have been written if not for Rev. Dr. Nicole B. Simpson, whom I happened to meet again in my first 10 months of freedom. I had the wonderful blessing of establishing an accountability partnership with her. In my 31st year of incarceration, I participated in a victim-focused program in which she was a guest speaker. Her powerful testimony impacted and impressed upon my thinking about myself in ways that I'm still unpacking.

Finally, I want to extend a special thank you to my sister, Tereasa, who has been an incredible foundation of support and source of inspiration for me during my reentry into a world I never truly could have known leaving as a kid. And to my Returning Citizen Support Group, let's keep changing the narrative!

Damon

Table of Contents

INTRODUCTION
FIERY RESURRECTIONS

"The white South said it knew 'niggers,' and I was what the white South called a 'nigger.' Well, the white South had never known me—never known what I thought, what I felt."
Richard Wright, 1945 edition of Black Boy.

I always imagined myself writing a book, but deep in my mind, I believed it was always just that, an imagination. I knew I wasn't prepared to meet the challenges of becoming a writer more than thirty years ago; it was too much work, too much reading. I dissuaded myself by believing I didn't have enough life experience to write anything that could hold someone's attention long enough to finish reading my story. However, that all changed when I met authors who had similar lived experiences and self-deprecating thoughts. It was them who showed me that not only do I have a story to tell, but I *mus*t tell it.

Now, thirty years later and after countless *fiery resurrections*, here are my printed boyhood memoirs and narrative. We must die many times to live our best possible lives. Parts of ourselves, our thinking, and our behaviors must be shed in order for our newer, wiser, and more learned selves to take root. A symbolic resurrection has to occur periodically in our lives in order for genuine, or authentic, growth to occur. Oftentimes, this transforming metaphysical growth will be painful, perhaps even excruciating: Maybe even torturous! But this fiery resurrection, as if a mythical Phoenix within, like any growth, requires a substantial sacrifice (cost). The cost for me is what I can only describe to you as - *A Beautiful Pain.*

To help you conceptualize what I mean by *A Beautiful Pain*, if you saw the movie *The Shawshank Redemption,* then begin to really, really imagine what it must have felt like for the character, Andy Dufresne, after he exited the putrid prison sewer waters in his struggling escape from his nightmarish prison. If you haven't seen this movie, I recommend you take time out of your life to watch (study) it. This is because any prison condition, whether physical or mental, can be nightmarish and I realized a long time ago that we're all in some form of personal imprisonment; and, that what matters most is: Are you willing to escape it, and if so, how much are you willing to sacrifice for agency? Are you willing to experience *A Beautiful Pain* for it?!

Richard Wright is arguably the writer who has had the most influence on my intellectual growth and development – basically, on my life! The "white South" he speaks about is the racialized system of oppression known as Jim Crow. His writings describe how living under Jim Crow was a constant existential battle for him to determine his agency and define his existence. But, more importantly, for me his writings illustrate how a subjugated people will reject the expectations, impositions, and false narratives placed on them by an oppressive society.

Mass incarceration has been described by some writers as this era's racialized system of oppression or racial-caste system (white South). Under any form of systemic oppression there are countless examples of human Will expressing its need to be and feel free through acts of rejection and aggression. Otherwise, under such conditions people are essentially imprisoned mentally, socially, personally, and physically. The existential battle evinced by Black and other marginalized youths in America's harshest cities during the time of my youth, unfortunately coincided with the mass incarceration project. They (we) experienced a double-imprisonment.

In the main, this book is about the various kinds of human imprisonment that most of these youths didn't fathom nor were even aware of being confined in. It is about my endeavor to utilize my past double-confinement in and liberation from these imprisonments as lessons for others to use as liberating guides from their own personal prisons. I felt there was a need to write this book because most people will find it extremely challenging to accept the possibility that they exist within a mental prison they've constructed on their own.

Storytelling is perhaps the most powerful edifying human tool ever created. And yet reading has become an anathema within the last couple of generations. One of my aims in writing this book, despite the current national abhorrence to reading, is using my story (which is the same story of so many system-impacted community members) to help individuals see past the veil of imposed false narratives.

Such a veil is actually a mental prison that limits one's ability to see their potential or their manifold possibilities. Thus, I share with the world what I learned from Richard Wright in order to free myself (the ransom for *A Beautiful Pain*) from the veil of ignorance, when he says - "It had been my accidental reading of fiction and literary criticism that had evoked in me glimpses of life's possibilities."

Flawed Perspectives at an Early Age

As an avid reader languishing inside a filthy New Jersey prison, I once read a philosopher's proposition that your present life is but an elaboration of your past. For me, this assertion reinforces a simple, yet poignant, notion: You are the sum total of choices you have made in your life. However, to that notion lest not forget, even the choices made in your childhood are included. What a frightening fact to process for many of us because our little brains had no clue about the painful and traumatic genealogy or root causes for making some dumbass choices. Even so, those choices (when you ruminate on them and the many ways, they affect you then and now) continue to elaborate (or enhance an understanding or idea of) your life. And as we all know, we can't talk about choices without talking about consequences. This becomes highly relevant in discussions involving Black existence that is immersed in a social world made of and ravaged by inequity and injustice - which limits the options of some people due to superficial human differences and produces an uneven distribution of socio-legal consequences in that society.

Specifically, socially unacceptable choices made by Black boys and girls in this country, who inherited far fewer options (and thus choices) than their White or affluent counterparts, incur substantially disproportionate consequences. These consequences originate from the long held American belief/myth that Black children are inherently irredeemable and therefore must be held to the same standard as that of any "shiftless" Black adult, and are a present reality in American social and legal institutions. Despite the fact that as human beings we all experience a developmental stage and can potentially grow into who we choose to become, Black children are constantly judged, fixed, as unchild-like, and treated accordingly. This explains why so many Black parents, as TaNehisi Coates alluded to in *The Beautiful Struggle*, experience a heightened sense of concern and fear when their Black boys are in their teenage years.

My story tells of this parental nightmare and puts it on full display from experiences in my childhood beginning in June 1980 when I was 11. The ordeal, one of many, was fully elaborated on only after decades of ritualized self-examination. This life-altering moment and traumatizing experience formed and directed the trajectory of my life. To help you fully understand it, I have textually leapt across temporal boundaries to make you an audience to my past experiences.

Back then, family and friends knew me to be curious, inquisitive, and to have an explorative mindset. I was that kid who was satisfied by taking hours of what I imagined as "conducting scientific and natural research" in exploring vacant lots that covered the landscape of my neighborhood. From the back porch of my family's two-and-a-half-family home in a poor, working-class section of Newark's west ward, I could clearly see about five blocks away from where I stood. The vacant lots that filled my neighborhood mirrored the aftermath of a war zone. These were the remnants of the Newark (New Jersey) riots in the late 60's.

I was oblivious to socio-political history and the reasons behind the eye sores (that's what adults back then called them) of vacant lots . We lived in abject poverty so we made the most of the environment our hood provided us. For me, the lots were my sanctuary, my laboratory, and my Shangri-la. The science and nature books I read as a child would inspire me to use the insects, creatures, and plant life I gathered from the vacant lots to earnestly attempt to identify a new or special species of some kind. In my mind, I wanted to earn national fame as a natural scientist. In my 11 year-old mind, I would gain recognition by sharing what I knew and what I liked doing with others. And if discovering an unfamiliar species could earn me acclaim, like biologist Charles Darwin did, then so be it!

At 11, I wasn't your typical shy kid. Yes, I was reserved but I "showed-out" as my mother would say whenever I got an audience. A career as a scientist or comedian was my goal during those years. My sense of humor was advanced for my age, too. I was so funny I'd have adults hugging their bellies in tears while laughing at something I said. Behind the laughter, I was hiding something terrible. I was getting bullied relentlessly. I can't pinpoint exactly when the bullying started but I clearly remember having to run home from school from time to time. Nothing physical, but the mere fact that groups of boys would chase me all the way home was daunting. And why did they bully me? Because girls in my class found me "cute," or teachers would praise me for participating in class by raising my hand, answering questions, and getting called to the board to demonstrate how to work a math problem. The intimidation that would come my way just for being cute and smart would traumatize me deeply, and negatively affect my self-image and confidence.

Now, let me be clear - *fighting* was never the problem; I could always fight and I was very good at it. But *I didn't like to fight* as a kid. I didn't want to hurt anyone. I didn't even want to fight those who poked fun at my tattered, hand me-down clothes, or even someone who actually tried to hurt me. The exact opposite was true - I knew how to hurt and cause people pain.

As a child, I was a very visual learner. If someone showed me how to do something once, I could figure out very easily how to do it on my own the next time. And, if it was shown to me twice, I mastered it! I watched fake-wrestling and Wide World of Sports boxing on a neighbor's television where I often spent time with a babysitter. I watched many hours of boxing and choreographed Greco-Roman wrestling in action. Rather than reenact what I learned and potentially harm someone, my personality had me hurl a joke rather than throw a punch in anger. I also didn't like experiencing pain and my 11-year-old self didn't want to be the cause of someone else's pain.

My desire not to fight was controlled by my inability to understand why I became a target for harassment and bullying in the first place. In hood terminology, getting dissed, chumped, or punked by other kids. I've since learned that my inability to engage in fighting stemmed from a serious, but not uncommon, emotional and intellectual imbalance. There was an uneven development of my emotional and intellectual capacities that favored the latter. EQ (emotional intelligence), as some researchers suggest, is the ability to recognize emotions within oneself and to use that awareness to guide one's decisions.[1] My EQ was very low. It made me become socially withdrawn, overly self-conscious and stressed. I began feeling out-of-control and detached from my own feelings - my own self. As a consequence of this persistent feeling I began to lose control of my emotions. I acted out in school, was disrespectful to adults and behaved in other ways expressive of a child in distress. I busted windows, touched girls' butts and vandalized property. Though I behaved this way, I could solve puzzles, math and reading problems while communicating and comprehending complex ideas for a child my age with ease. My intelligence had me rarely get caught for my misbehavior. Even with all this, trying to understand the negative and disruptive emotional reactions directed at me by other kids confused the heck out of me. It debilitated me emotionally.

In hindsight, I believe the confusion resulted from my semi-sheltered early childhood. I remember spending many of my formative years socially alone, not around other kids. If I found myself outside around other children, they were too young to be

---

[1] Goleman, Daniel. *Emotional Intelligence.*

playmates. So I was usually not very far from my mother growing up. Bernadine Gilliam Venable gave birth to her first child, my brother, Marvin Jr., at age 15, shortly after marrying my father. She gave birth to me, her second child, at age 18. At 21, my sister, Vanita, was born, and some years later, Tereasa and Trunetta, my younger sisters, joined us.

My mother would lovingly recount that I was a shy, reserved, and quiet kid. I was also a daydreamer and lover of sleep. I rarely cried, complained, or bothered her. She would describe countless times that when I was a baby and toddler, she would spontaneously get concerned about me and check the room I was in because I was so quiet for extended periods of time. She'd jokingly say, "He was my best baby because he slept all day and rarely cried when he was awake." Because of my quietude, though, my mother developed a subtle protectiveness over me. It would keep me in her company. She was a stay-at-home young mother. As such, she introduced me to gossip, news, and other affairs just so she could have a social outlet. Perhaps due to her own sheltered life, I was brought into mature topics and became familiar with adult social mores and knowledge far beyond my years. My daydreamer's imagination would have me craft my own analysis and conclusions about the things I didn't understand.

(As I reflect back, for a young boy this was *not* a good thing! In my adulthood, I've learned the importance of seeking guidance when forming my view of things from different knowledge sources. Doing this serves as a light in the darkness of our understanding. When we're left to our own thinking, personal and emotional influences, predispositions or bents, advice and instruction from others help develop a more balanced and objective outlook.)

Through this daydreamer's lens, as a child, my outlook on the world and myself became skewed. My hasty introduction into an adult social sphere at this early age, while sheltered from my peer group in my formative years, led to the confusion. As a kid, I was socially unskilled but physically tough and mentally resilient - up to a point. That point was the threshold of when the violence began. My emotional confusion progressed and it would usher in physical altercations, and the fist-fighting period of my life commenced during my early-middle school years.

Before the youthful period of my fighting crusades, my natural fight or flight response was set firmly on flight. I guess that explains why I was gifted with speedy legs. (I remember when at the park, on a dare, I'd race and beat track runners who trained religiously.) My instincts were set on avoidance and retreat but one day this changed in a drastic way.

One day my brother witnessed me getting chased home - bullied. He responded in the way big brothers did in the hood, he ran them off with a kick in the butt and some harsh words:

"I'mma make my little brother fuck ya'll up the next time I see ya'll." Hearing those words caused a sharp, cutting pain down my back. I felt each word with such brutality, I thought I heard my spine crackle as it happened. My insides coiled-up like a frightened boa constrictor when I heard my brother's promise of me exacting vengeance on them.

At that moment I was ready to run away from home to anywhere, any place because I knew what was to come. My brother meant those words and he intended to turn them into facts. And I was going to be the facilitator of those facts whether or not I wanted to be. Why? Because the other option was even more traumatizing. "Goddamn, goddamn!" - is all I kept saying in my head. The agony, the extreme crisis I experienced from the impending upheaval in my 11 year-old world had emotionally ripped me asunder, shredded my innocence and snatched-out the core fiber of my being. It felt like I was unmade that day.

My brother is three years older than me and cut from the same cloth as our father. Our dad was that tough, rough and thorough class of man who didn't back down from an invitation to fight. He would throw-down anywhere, anytime with anyone. Meanness exuded from him like danger and death radiates from rattlesnakes and king cobras. Backing down from a fight was morally reprehensible to both my dad and brother. To do so was cowardly; it was just downright unmanly. (I must have forgotten to ask for that gene when I was conceived. I've always been a bit absent-minded like that, even in the womb it appears my head was in the clouds.) I felt so unlike them - an embarrassment. This shame is what allowed me to comfortably keep my being bullied a secret from them.

But the day my brother made that pronouncement, my secret was no more. My big brother, that thorough, light-skinned, red-haired kid with a bigtime rep in our hood just found out his little brother was getting punked and bullied. Stressful feelings overwhelmed my mind as we walked home. My senses were numbed for a while. It was like death himself punched the shit outta me. Strangely, I could only hear my brother's contemptuous criticisms and reproaches. I knew his words should have hurt me, but I felt nothing as I heard what he had to say. What I felt was clear - that the revelation about my cowardice would be the start of a new approach to life I would have to take whether I like it or not. My life would be burdened with this and challenged in a way I hadn't experienced nor expected. What my brother declared was contrary to my personality and, more importantly, opposite of the me I wanted to be.

Everything between the world and me, as I knew it, was going to change after this day. "The Talk" was on the horizon and I wasn't ready for it.

The me I wanted to be was an aspiring comedian and scientist. Though I possessed a deep sense of insecurity and introvertedness, the "Talk" was about to make me replace my persona with that of my brother's and father's. The anxiety I experienced from thinking about this imminent transition was psychologically paralyzing.

I remember clearly the moment my incensed brother and I finally arrived home. My intent was to make a bee-line straight for my room and plunk myself on the bed, when I heard my brother ask my mother, "When is daddy coming home?"

My mom replied, "In a few hours. Why?"

"Because your son is letting people bully him and chase him home."

"DAMON DONNELLE, come here!", my mother called out, sternly but lovingly.

"Oh damn!," I faintly murmured to myself as I thought, "Even mommy is upset with me."

Anyone else could be disappointed with my actions and I wouldn't give too much a damn about it. But her? My sweet mother? The one who always had encouraging words towards me? The one who was patient with my unrealized potential in spite of my persistent faults and mischievous indiscretions? For her to be ashamed of me or angry at me for being a punk made me feel deeply low. "Just kill me now, Lord!" - I cried to the Heavens.

In obedience, I moped into the kitchen with a slumped back. My eyes ogled at the floor as I met her in the kitchen. "Yes, Mom," I replied dryly.

"What is your brother talking about?" she said with so much concern and compassion. I immediately recognized that she wasn't a tad bit disappointed. She was both secretly, but noticeably, examining me to see if I was injured and also gauging my emotional state. "What is your brother talking about, I asked you?" she firmly repeated.

"Some boys were picking on me," I said unconvincingly.

She hollered, "Why?"

"I don't know," I replied weakly and dishonestly. Deep down, I knew they bullied me because of my reluctance to fight, and my low self-esteem and feelings of low self-worth didn't help. The fact that I was constantly bullied by groups and never just one person made me run, too.

"Are you okay?" my mother asked authoritatively.

"Yes."

"Those boys on 16th Avenue messing with you again?" she asked with a shrewd tone. I was stunned! She knew! But how? I wasn't going to lie to her - though I wanted to. Lying had become second nature to me by then.

"Yes, it was them," I confessed with embarrassment.

"Well, you ain't hurt so you did something right. Thank God. But you can't keep letting people bully and scare you; they'll never stop doing it. You know you have cousins on 16th Avenue on your father's side, right? Maybe you should talk to them."

Then she added, "You know what your father's going to do about this when he gets home, right?"

Those were her last words on the subject. I just nodded my head and walked towards the room my brother and I shared. He was already there.

Boom! My left rib cage was met with a right hook as soon as I stepped through our bedroom door. My brother landed the blow. The sound from the contact he made with my tender 11-year-old ribs resembled in tone, pitch and power to the thumps in the movie, *Rocky*, when Sylvester Stallone's character punched the beef carcasses in the butcher shop's freezer in preparation for his fight.

I folded over with my left arm covering the violated section of my torso. I knew better than to wince or shriek in pain. I took the blow silently but with anger. I'd cry about it when I was alone but not now.

"Since you gonna let chumps punk you, I might as well get mine too if you givin' out freebies and ain't gonna fight back," my brother said sarcastically. It sounded like he was trying to inspire me but it wasn't working.

Seconds later we both heard dad's old Ford pick-up truck pull-up in front of the house. My brother bolted out the door to meet him. I was wildly imagining what that conversation sounded like. At that moment I just stood in the middle of the room wholly incapable of physical movement between our twin beds. Overwhelmed, stressed and wanting to vanish I heard the rumble of the hallway's floorboard. My father's feet, carrying all of his 240 pounds, entered the apartment. Surprisingly, he went into his bedroom, where my mother was, and closed the door.

"Damn, he's getting his belt," I exclaimed to myself quietly. "Who the fuck beats their kid for getting chased home, anyway?" - I said, trying to pep-talk myself any way I could.

I heard my parent's bedroom door open and I heard my father's voice say, "And it's the same boys chasing him? He's not fighting back, just running from them?"

My mother said something in response but I couldn't hear it.

"DAMON DONNELLE," my father yelled. His tone was *way* different from my mother's. It was a summons for me to present myself to him immediately. I freed myself from my paralysis and approached the living room where my father and brother were standing. When I entered, my father said, "We're all gonna have a talk. This will be the only time we'll talk about this. You understand?"

I didn't answer him because his question was rhetorical. He went on: "You got two choices Damon Donnelle. You start fighting those boys picking on you and anybody else trying to bully you or, and you don't want this alternative, you'll have to fight me and your brother if you don't fight back. And after that you'll go and fight them boys. So do you want one fight or two fights? Your choice. So what are you going to do?"

"One fight," I meekly responded.

"Alright then, go clean yourself up and get ready to eat," he casually answered. Upon my answering of one fight, I saw my brother nodding his head in great anticipation, approval and glee. I was saying to myself, as I saw the look of battle-lust on his face, "What the hell is HE so happy about?" And just like that "The Talk" that I dreaded was over. But the ramifications of it would linger. That day of "The Talk" marked the creation of a young danger to society - the violent juvenile-offender I would become.

The Talk's Aftermath

I've learned one thing about a traumatic incident - when suffering it you don't always know that 1.) it is a traumatic incident; and 2.) that it will potentially reverberate negatively throughout your life as behavior driven by formative experiences. Your conscious attention is mostly focused on surviving the ordeal. Depending on the degree of pain and life-threatening conditions, individuals consciously disassociate (or disconnect) their minds from their bodies while the traumatic incident is unfolding. Think of it as a mental or emotional circuit-breaker. It's the mind's fail-safe that shuts some of its parts down to protect itself. Therein lies the core of traumatic experiences. Parts of us get temporarily shut down for survival purposes and those parts never get turned back on. If they do, we're not guaranteed to be the same as we were before it all happened. The person suffering trauma is altered on a consciousness level, and without proper guidance, counseling, support and encouragement, no degree of inner resiliency or high intelligence alone can completely counteract its effects or alterations to a person's psyche.

"The Talk" represents a significant and pivotal point in my life. It was an absolutely traumatic experience for me. The emotional and cognitive damage it exacted on my adolescent psyche was scarring and horrific. It stunted me emotionally, socially, and in other ways I'm still grappling with this late in life. For me, "The Talk" would become a powerful inner gravitation that not only pulled me into a world of communicating through violence but it also made the language, the feel, the movement, and the power of violence appear sexy, cool and attractive.

Combining this hypnotic-like force of violence with my emotional underdevelopment, and feeling as though I was left to my own healing devices and self-correcting measures, my misguided path was conceived. It didn't help that I grew-up alongside other traumatized kids in an impoverished neighborhood during the trickle-down economic policy years of the Reagan presidency. There was no therapeutic counseling from family services. My smarts and resiliency easily morphed into a dysfunction while living life through a selfish, hurt and frightened perspective.

I believe that children don't have the capacity to have a clear perspective on anything besides their own basic desires at that moment. This makes childhood trauma not only devastating for the child, but dangerous for those with whom they come in contact because children will often time behaviorally produce what is happening to them. Additionally, society can suffer if a child is hurting and that child learns to communicate his hurt by way of hurting others.

My own dysfunction took place during the course of the years immediately following "The Talk" with my father and brother. Traumatic events can happen in one quick moment, many quick and successive moments, or over an extended period of time. These events can happen independently and interdependently of each other; a convergence of sufferings.

The environment I grew up in surrounded me with utter scarcity. Societal issues alongside systemic racism and economic disparity had many people - children included - reject the thought that abiding by the dominant culture's morals was necessary to succeed in life. My little mind was bombarded by societal pressures and socio-cultural forces that were beyond my conscious awareness or ability to understand. I, like so many other Black boys, had normalized my trauma. I seemed to be at the point of no return in developing a dysfunctional mindset while, unknowingly, beginning to exhibit nihilistic tendencies.

(Nihilism is a desire to reject established norms, values and systems. It's having a belief that life has no ultimate meaning or purpose. Later in life I discovered that nihilistic thoughts and attitudes were attractive to me because I believed society rejected me. That it disregarded my feelings. I would later discover that this is an issue countless Black writers have written about. Most notably, Richard Wright, author of *Black Boy* and *Native Son*, has poignantly captured this phenomena of American white society assuming to know Black folk without ever knowing or caring what we thought or how we feel.)

I was already socially inept and emotionally underdeveloped and so my mind became fertile soil for the cultivation of an antisocial personality. I became emotionally detached from the world and from others. An inner, self-destructive process of emotional unhinging took place. I didn't know it at the time because my child mindset was just that - a young, innocent and developing mind that not too long ago was thrown in as a Being-in-the-world. I inexplicably veered from becoming a positive Being to a callous person, and it ultimately showed itself. Childhood is a time in which positive growth and meaning are supposed to be the primary orientation. It's also the period in which mistakes abound in a human being's development.

Adolescent years can be a time of rebelliousness, madness, and indifference - a transitory stage in our lives highlighting self-discovery as we navigate through just beingness-in-the-world and our immediate environment. But when trauma intercedes this transitory stage, as it did for me, external factors begin shaping and influencing every developing aspect of childhood. Bad children are not born, they are made. They're made by environments from which they cannot remove themselves. In existential psychology (the study of our existence), being is meant to become a state rather than just an activity, while the world in human life means more than just the environment, see (N., Sam M.S., "BEING-IN-THE-WORLD," in *PsychologyDictionary.org*, April 7, 2013, https://psychologydictionary.org/being-in-the-world/ (accessed June 26, 2022). Philosophy of Martin Heidegger). My childhood experiences, and my responses to them, would eventually have me perceive life as an activity of personal retribution and not as a state of peaceful co-existence with others.

What are the chances of a child developing normally in subpar school-to-prison pipeline education systems, the deluge of drugs and its rampant use were (and still are) prevalent; and add to this, race-based, aggressive over-policing while immersed in a state of wretched financial deprivation and abysmal living conditions? Situated in such an environment psychologically conditioned by systemic oppressive tendencies and lacking sufficient resources, its negative contributions and impact on my and so many other youths' dysfunctional expressions make sense. Like so many Black boys and girls, I had to experience this compounding trauma on a daily basis. It was persistent. Many of us failed to get through this by unconsciously allowing our psyche to identify with the negative aspects of our environment, social disadvantages and the stigmatizations of our trauma.

I believe nihilistic spaces were deliberately constructed for the Black population from anti-Black beliefs and practices by white ruling society. In no way do I share this as a conspiracy theory or an attempt to shirk personal responsibility. American history is well-documented with redlining as a practice in financial institutions, lynching, segregation of all kinds, gerrymandering, and neoliberalism. Specifically, neoliberalism is the divisive and totalizing oppressive force that continues to ravage our Black communities. It’s a throwback to Reagan-era economic policies. Those policies deregulated banking institutions and relaxed many legal constraints on powerful, rich corporations under the premise that if the government allowed the "Rich Class" unfettered access to make profits, then these profits would "trickle down" the social-economic strata in American society. This economic policy produced both a serious financial blowback onto Black life, which was already trapped in economically lacking spaces. This, too, contributed mightily to the dysfunctionality of the Black community, its families, and individuals, like me.

History documents how this deep-rooted communal dysfunctionality produced a significant amount of clientele for the mass incarceration project. For those with highly compulsive personalities and unsteady psyches, this era was devastating. The federal government pumped cheap, addictive drugs in poor Black communities. These neighborhoods experienced crisis-level rates of diagnosed mental disorders while many went undiagnosed. People who were impacted by persistent drug use found themselves rejecting the establishment's ways of living a so-called peaceful, orderly life, its values and principles in pursuit of their next high. The human condition of Black and impoverished people were promoted as worthless. I found myself, and others found themselves, trying to counter this belief and empower ourselves through what we thought was our only means - socially unacceptable behavior. Criminality, violence and drug use became our norm. These perils were viewed as acts of retribution but the cause was so much deeper.

As I reflect on my childhood, the aftermath of "The Talk" was just as, if not more, traumatizing than "The Talk" itself. Figuratively, the aftermath started the countdown toward an emotional time bomb that would eventually explode. In my panicked emotional state, the looming threat of violence in the neighborhood had just been overtaken by a more serious and imminent threat of violence. This new threat of violence, I incorrectly perceived, came from within my own home, my supposed sanctuary and safe space.

No longer would I worry as much about the punk kids in the neighborhood that I essentially emboldened because I chose to run from them. Hell, I could outrun Bruce Jenner and Wild Boy on a bad day (so I believed…)! But I couldn't outrun my own brother who slept in the same room or a father who had complete authority over me. From that day my mind became an anxiety factory. I constantly worried about getting punished for even the slightest perceived "diss" or "punk" from a neighborhood kid if my brother spotted me doing nothing about it.

My anxiety also birthed a gradual fascination for weapons. I even began making my own. I went from catching grasshoppers and lightening bugs in jars one summer to making "nigga-be-kool-sticks" and karate nunchucks the next summer. Though the transition of becoming comfortable with violence or resolving conflicts with violence didn't happen quickly, I spent my days preparing for it. For a time I was still more inclined to avoid and evade, but I now had to do it either without being seen by my brother or family or doing it without "losing face." Soon, the inner distress would negatively impact my academic performance. I developed a disdain for school. I hated it there because that's where most of the bullying and harassment took place.

Before the bullying, getting an education was never an issue for me. I loved learning. It was the construct of the school that was the problem. The social dynamic confused and overwhelmed me. Once I figured out that my eagerness to raise my hand in class and solve problems at the board were qualities that bullies targeted in their prey, I abstained from participating. I slowly embarked on a dumbing-down campaign in an attempt to be left alone. This change wouldn't go unnoticed by a teacher or two. They didn't try to figure out why either. For example, I remember my 6th-grade teacher calling on me to answer problems at the board more than five times. After a while, she said in a perturbed tone, "Okay, Damon, it seems a cat has suddenly got your tongue because your homework assignment I graded says you know the answer, but alright ..."

School gradually became a very uncomfortable place. I couldn't figure out what to do to change that. As much as I loved learning, the environment was hostile, threatening and made me feel awkward. Feeling like prey made me not want to be there. Bitterness developed from my powerlessness of not having a say. This bitterness would spawn in a deep dislike for school, authority and education. It marked the beginning of disconnecting from acceptable ways of behavior (nihilism). I became withdrawn emotionally. I was hollow inside. I became a good actor and a consummate liar. Many adults noticed my slow descent into being "a bad child". Elders in the neighborhood and family noticed what teachers had noticed, too. The joke-telling, smiley-faced kid they knew was now acting differently. Simple things began to catch their attention - not acknowledging them with a courteous greeting when walking by, becoming verbally expressive using expletives, demonstrating aggressive and abusive tendencies, not turning in homework, fighting in school, destroying property and, most noticeably, hanging out with bad company.

When family members or community elders would approach me about my new behaviors, I heard them but did not listen. My ways did not change. I would let my creative imaginations produce, and accept, a convenient untruth. At the same time, I would refuse to acknowledge that I was changing my ways. I kept this inner dilemma hidden and silent because I was afraid, ashamed and - most of all - embarrassed. Within myself I capitulated and watched as I became some "thing" other than what I wanted to become. I accepted being powerless and chose weakness as my guide.

As a boy I characterized myself as "a let down," because I wasn't like my father or brother. I didn't have a ferocious nature that radiated from my aura that made people respect me and fear me at the same time. I was consumed by toxic shame that emanated from believing I was responsible for everything bad that happened to me. I blamed myself. My low-level of self-worth would inevitably infect all other aspects of my being. I encountered bullies and their hostility constantly during 7th grade. Their abuse wore me down. A simple walk to the bathroom during class would easily erupt into a fist fight in the boy's restroom. I knew boys who wouldn't even use the restroom in middle school. They'd "hold it" until lunchtime or wet their pants. I had my limits though.

On particularly good days in school I was rewarded with a 10-minute comedy session by my teacher when the circumstances were ripe. When the teacher wanted a laugh or a break from the classroom, I'd get approval to tell jokes. One time I told some Richard Pryor jokes complete with a little neighborhood lingo and visuals. I cracked myself up that day. Things were good on days like this but a rarity during these times.

"Alright Damon, I need my class back," she would say in jest. Jokes were over.

"May I go to the bathroom first?" I asked respectfully. She agreed.

I remember walking to the bathroom through the halls of Fifteenth Avenue School. My class was on the 2nd floor, at the back of the school. I recall saying to myself, "I hope the 2nd floor bathroom is open." I didn't want to walk to the first floor bathroom near the front of the building. Sometimes it was the only bathroom open because the principal wanted to decrease the malevolence taking place inside of them throughout the building and that bathroom was near his office. The proximity of the bathroom to the highest authority figure in the school really didn't matter to predatory-minded kids. In fact, that bathroom was ground-zero for most of the unkind acts against children by other children.

On this particular day I had to go to the first floor bathroom. I was in a rush, because I was holding a gallon of Pepsi inside my bladder that turned into urine. I kicked the bathroom door open and made my way to a urinal. I heard someone in the stall yell out, "Who the fuck kicking the door like that?" Reflexively, I thunderously blurted out, "Me, motherfucker!"

"Who's me?," the voice calmly and confidently asked.

My thunderous blurt was an oddity and not the norm because I wasn't the type to provoke fights. At this point in life my temperament was still on the modest-side despite having defended myself in some one-on-one altercations quite a few times. The reality of the hood, and my confidence as a good fighter, compelled me to "rock out" in a fair fight match. It was the cadre of bullies that triggered the fear of death or flight in me. Or, the duke of the neighborhood with the fiercest rep who would send quakes of fear down my spine. I thought these guys, who I believe were much like my brother and father, had discovered the secrets of living stress free and unworried in the hood.

"Damon!" I delivered in a proud and firm voice to the mysterious guy in the bathroom stall. It felt good to meet that diss with confidence. The mystery guy's voice gave-off a sound that sent needles through my veins - he sucked his teeth. That sound is a contemptuous, disrespectful gesture anywhere. Whether the hood, suburb or corporate room, the sound of sucking teeth means you're not fazed or bothered by what the other person just said. For a split second my confidence was rattled but something new came over me. I was tired of being possessed by fear of other people. I was tired of being weak and powerless. "This shit is going to stop," I said to myself to boost my confidence.

After what seemed like an eternity for me, I instinctively blurted out, "Yeah, fuck you too - whoever you are!" The words that bellowed from behind that stall next would seemingly re-traumatize me for a flash.

"I'll see you Damon, this Nut," the voice said so passively and almost kindly.

I didn't immediately think that Nut's response elicited any fear. In hindsight, why wasn't he afraid? Why wouldn't he be afraid while sitting on the toilet - as vulnerable as can be? I missed that strategic advantage because I was so paralyzed by the magnitude of the violence that awaited me. Nut was the school's number-one feared dude. His style of dress was bummy and dirty couture, and he wore it proudly. I won't call him a bully because he didn't harass people who he felt were weaker than him or different and wouldn't fight back. Nut was a grade or two behind and looked like a grown man in the 8th grade. "What the hell did I just get myself into?"- I nervously questioned myself.

I remember an emotional composure settling on me and spurring me to claim to myself, "Fuck it! Nut rocks by himself anyway. If I get my ass whooped in a fair one, what can my father and brother say to me." "I'll be in the playground after school," I said loudly before exiting the bathroom. I thought to myself, "I was going to fight Nut today," as I walked back to my class. I wasn't nervous. And that surprised me the most. I looked at the clock only once. Didn't need to keep looking at it, my mind went somewhere else. I was lost in my imagination. I was transforming into Muhummad Ali and Sugar Ray Leonard for the epic middle school fracas that was about to go down with me as the great underdog.

I was driven out of my daydream by the rumbling of the school bell. I packed my books in the desk, "Fuck homework, I got a fight to go to," I anxiously told myself. I walked towards the playground. Nothing unusual or no large crowds there. But as I turned inside the gate to it, there he stood amid a few spectators. "How'd they know?"- I thought. I didn't tell anyone. I was incensed by his public announcement when I could've bragged but I didn't. "The disrespect! He must think I'm going to be easy" - I howled inwardly. Well, I wasn't that day.

Nut bested me but it was a pyrrhic victory for him. He won the fight, knocked me down and dragged me like a rag doll around that playground. While getting dragged by this monstrous man-child, I remember thinking - "He's fucking up my favorite pair of Swedish Knits pants." Surprisingly I had very few scars and not one on my face. If you weren't at that fight you would have thought Nut was the loser at first glance. His eye was swollen. His nose was busted and he had a deep scar on his forehead. I was ferocious that day, and it came through me in a natural and calm way. I wasn't scared but I was in semi-control of my emotions. I was thinking as the fight took place. I wasn't worried about a loss, my brother or my father. When I used a jagged brick's edge to slam against Nut's forehead, exacting a deluge of blood, I remember wondering what my mother was going to think if she knew I was hurting someone like this. I often had inner monologues at the weirdest times.

The fight unceremoniously came to an end after someone yelled, "Won't ya'll stop!" Nut had me in a headlock trying to choke me out, but I wouldn't let him get both of his hands clasped to deliver the strength needed to cut-off my air supply. He was bloody, we were tired, and he finally let me go after the spectator's plea to stop the fight. He stood up first, then me. I looked him in his eyes and said, "We ain't gotta stop!" The look on his face was of absolute dismay. My statement was a gambit. I looked at him and knew he was hurting badly. I wanted another shot at him, though. I wanted one more crack at the duke of the school and I was sure I'd beat him. And if he declined it would be a symbolic victory for me.

I was able to gamble. I was a light-skinned, pretty boy - an underdog - without an ounce of threatening aura. He couldn't decline my offer. If he did so, he would lose face (or cool points). But then, a spectator's voice shouted out, "Go ahead, lil' Rah (my brother's street name)! You represented. Let it go, y'all aight." And before I could respond, Nut dejectedly turned around and began walking towards 16th Avenue. I watched him walk until he hit the avenue. I was almost hoping he'd have a sudden mind to do an about-face. He walked without the slightest gesture of turning around. So I went home, less than a block away.

When I got there I sat on the porch and began crying uncontrollably. It was an intense, spastic, sudden physical affliction. It resembled a cinematic scene where a person undergoes an excruciating mutation into a supernatural beast. But this imaginative resemblance isn't just figurative; I painfully transformed into someone other than my mother's child then.

"The Talk" with my father and brother, though traumatic and emotionally pivotal in my life, brought me to the precipice of an abyss - the edge of a pit. The experience undoubtedly disconnected me from my authentic self and the most positive trajectory of my life. My fight with Nut, a figure representing the benefits and effectiveness of violence as a means of communication, would be the event that pushed me off the edge deep into the pit of darkness and violence—my new reality.

Lessons I Should Have Learned From My Father

The biggest misconception I had about my father and brother is that they were violent individuals. My father would rather berate you or scare you into correction (although he would lay a pop on you with the quickness if you crossed his line of intolerance). The looming threats of violence from my father were bluffs. They were meant to get me past my own fears and insecurities. I didn't know this about my father at the time. Unfortunately, I learned too late.

My father was born in Virginia in 1945. He dropped out of school in the 3rd grade to become a "full-time country boy," as he would say with a smile. Education was not a priority at the time he grew up. Having food and money to take care of the family was. Times were difficult then, so dad and his brothers all left school to help the family sustain a living. Eventually, they all migrated to New Jersey in the late 1950s. Although my father had no formal education and couldn't read, his entrepreneurial acumen and hustle made him a provider. Was he financially well-off? No, but he kept a roof over his family's head and food on the table even during the toughest of economic times. He possessed a great but quiet wisdom. My father also had a serious quality about him that caused people to either fear or like him, or both.

I witnessed my dad transform into an individual who spoke with violence during minor traffic incidents. Before road-rage was a thing, my dad mastered it. One time a drunk driver tapped my dad's truck ever so lightly with no scratch to be found. My father exploded with anger toward the driver while my brother and I witnessed it all from the car. All verbal. No fisticuffs. My father was a laborer and stayed in laborer clothing. And he was a big man. His presence was intimidating. The man gave my father $200 for the trouble. When my father got in the car, he gave a firm instruction, "Never let anyone get away with shit. You do it once, you'll keep letting 'em do it."

He wasn't just a talker either. While accompanying him on a home repair job in an affluent Essex County, New Jersey neighborhood, I saw him grab the homeowner's throat with both hands. The heavy-set Italian man claimed he didn't have the money to pay my father for the job right then. Shortly following the exchange of a few words, while still being choked, the homeowner miraculously and generously handed my father more than he owed.

Both of these incidents instilled a fear in me. My brother would always mock me for it and my dad would just reinforce the same - "Never let people take advantage of you; they'll never stop" - speech. Dad would demonstrate many examples where conflict resolution didn't involve actual violence but a convincing, strong display of its potential.

I missed the meaning of these experiences back then but not my brother. Rah would learn how to effectively deploy all forms of violent communications as a conflict resolution strategy. At the pinnacle of his violent engagement as a teenager, my brother developed a reputation as someone who will "put in work." Putting in work is street colloquialism that describes someone who has no qualms about fighting or fighting with weapons (bats, knives, pipes, etc.). While playing with my bat and ball one summer, I witnessed my brother get revenge on a guy with whom he had "an open account" (a beef). My brother snuck up on me and snatched the bat. As he cuffed the fat part of the bat in his hand and let the shaft ride along his arm, he peeked around the corner of a building. I knew what was about to happen but the target of the beef had no clue.

As his intended target exited the store and headed up the street, my brother tip-toed behind him, let the bat slide down his arm, he gripped it tightly and swung backwards. The guy turned around too late and got cracked in the back of his head! The swing was the most powerful I had seen directed at a human being. The contact put the guy out immediately.

The summertime crowds of people witnessed this near fatal act of violence in complete horror. I was in shock. I stayed there, hoping the victim got up and didn't die. In those moments, I was fearful and concerned about my brother's fate. I could care less about the guy on the ground since my brother said that, “he put his hands on me when he had numbers (he was around his boys) a while back at a party.” I was a spectator of some grotesque acts of violence in my neighborhood. And watching my brother and father navigate through it prompted an emotional response that made me know clearly that I wasn’t like them. I couldn’t live up to their standards, actions and expectations. My world was an emotional paradox - a huge contradiction. My non-violent predisposition was surrounded by violent prone individuals. I remember having a sense of urgency that this contradiction had to be resolved, quickly.

Amidst the violent interactions, some of my fondest memories of my father are our many fishing trips and the countless times he’d take my brother and I on repair jobs. My father was a mason by profession but also a jack of many other skilled trades, i.e. mechanics, plumbing, carpentry, and more. He was a natural teacher and taught by example. Since those times I have developed a great love and admiration for my father. When I was a child, though, I didn’t like him. Oftentimes felt uncomfortable around him. He wasn’t a talker.

Instead, he was an action-oriented person. It was difficult for me to gauge my father on any level and that made him a stranger to me. This tormented my mind.

The strangeness of my father, a primary male role model in my life, was simultaneously a sheer mystery that would wreak havoc on my mind. The psychological destruction it created would lead me to the constant misreading and misinterpretation of my father's instructions and living examples he was displaying. I was reacting and responding to him in ways that I thought or assumed he desired. For example, he was adamant about his sons and daughters standing up for themselves; "being tough people in a tough world," as he said often. I'd eventually interpret that as being someone who would easily resort to violence to resolve a problem. I was so wrong!

My father never advocated violence as a predominant conflict resolution skill. I would miss that principle completely. As I look back on my life, I misread his invaluable insights and instructions because of two critically important factors: 1) my own emotional faults or delayed emotional development, and 2) my being socially immersed in a violent, poverty-stricken environment (urban war zone) that caused me to assimilate to and socialize me under hostile circumstances. Violence became my default predisposition. My flight or fight response was moving solely towards fight. My surprising change into a fierce, callous, and selfish youth who moved only by inner hurt, pain and confusion had begun.

The Wrong Side of Town

During the summer of 7th grade, I remember feeling paralyzing fear when my mother called for me as I played outside. She gave me $3 to purchase chop meat for dinner from 303 Meat Market. Mom sternly told me, "Go now!" The meat market happened to be on 16th Avenue. In anger I thought, "goddam!" I had to go on an unnegotiable mission through enemy territory. It was near 4:30pm, too, so I knew there was a 99% chance that 16th Avenue was active and bustling with its social predators.

My mind went into military preparation mode. In an instant, I went from playfully figuring out how to throw a ball or tag another kid, to thinking about what kind of weapon to carry or how to rally up a group of bodies that'll be ready to throw-down on my behalf. A weapon was the option. I didn't have a ride-or-die partner or friend at the time. That friend who had your back because of a pact you formed over the years. That kind of pact had terms that are unconsciously understood and socially formed through years of dependable and physical support.

Since I was socially a loner, I was perceived as socially unfamiliar and inept among my peers. It was difficult to broker alliances for wartime action and assistance. Since a weaponized defense strategy was my only option, I went to the basement of my house. This location became my armory and weapons workshop. All my father's trade tools were at my disposal. This laboratory and sanctuary was a space that fed my creative resourcefulness. I'd spend most of my summer days alone in this workshop building go-karts and bikes. I fixed things in the house for my mother, repaired broken televisions, radios and electric toys. I honed my craft so well, my father would give me assignments to fix things on the family cars.

After time, I developed the world vision of an engineer or architect from a simple answer my father gave to me. I asked him how he had learned and mastered fixing so many things. His reply was, "Just remember how you take the thing apart and if there's pieces leftover when you put it back together, then you know you did something wrong."

That simple jewel of wisdom sent me running straight toward my fullest potential. I had gained the courage to explore the art of fixing things. As a result, I overcame my fears of failure and sense of low self-worth. "I'm fucking good at doing this stuff," I remember saying to myself one day after tinkering with a record player I found in the trash and fixed. Regretfully, this courage didn't translate into other positive views and actions. The loss of translation would become a central reason for my eventual waywardness. Once the need to navigate the hostile social environment at my doorstep arose, I had to simultaneously encounter and adjust to a brand new set of street values and norms.

Survival and personal safety in this war zone's neighborhood encampment would become an imperative. In philosophical terms, a moral imperative is "an absolute, unconditional necessity that must be obeyed in all circumstances and is justified as an end in itself," see (https://en.wikipedia.org/wiki/Categorical_imperative). The zone of aggression that surrounded me threatened me to the point that I adopted an absolute, unconditional obligation to meet aggression with aggression; my own imperative. This view became an instrumental part of my value system. My well-regarded intrinsic values were still very much present in me but they would unfortunately cease to be a pivotal source of personal motivation.

I still needed to get the chop meat by venturing into rival land. At the most basic level, mommy needed to cook dinner before dad came home. I remember sizing-up different weapons - knives, sticks, pipes and blow torches (I made cans of flammable sprays with a lighter that was duct-taped near the nozzle) in my arms depot down in the basement. Deciding which one would be appropriate for my mission to the meat store that would certainly end in a violent encounter was difficult. The other option was to amass a posse but I didn't want to bother my cousins who lived in that neighborhood. I had learned they were younger than me by only a couple of years. Worrying about them during hostile activity was a distraction I didn't need. At that moment it hit me. I decided that since I knew how to fight I would simply go unarmed but ready to fight.

I went to the meat store and across the street was a group of kids my age. I knew them from school. They spotted me and I eye-balled them back as I went into the store. “It’s about to go down,” I thought to myself. When I gave the butcher my order, I asked for it to be double-wrapped. I couldn’t risk losing the meat to a torn bag once the fighting began. Then, I looked out the store’s front window to see only two of the boys from the group waiting for me. I placed the bag of meat in the waistband of my jeans and tied it securely.

I walked out the store only to see the two boys walking back across the street. I didn’t question their retreat. I went home.

Years later, in 10th grade, I learned why the two boys walked away from the store. One of the guys who remained across the street, Kareem, and I became friends in high school. At the time of the chop meat run, we weren’t friends but had no beef either. During a conversation we reminisced about the 303 Meat Market event. He said the reason why the two boys decided not to confront me was that, “They saw you tucking the bag in your pants, like you were preparing to "put in work." In that conversation I knew that this attitude and the unquestionable readiness to "throw down" and meet aggression with aggression solidified my social makeover in the neighborhood.

By the time 8th grade was over, I was hanging out in West Side Park whenever I wanted. This was a big deal because to get to the park I had to walk through 16th Avenue. The park was still enemy territory. I hung out in the park longing for a battle. The appeal of violence was now coming from an internal source - my new mindset. I learned to welcome its invitation as an opportunity to prove myself and measure my fighting abilities. To what and whom I wanted to prove? The answer: a set of dysfunctional norms, beliefs and values as represented by the individuals in that dysfunctional space. I discovered that if I spoke through violence it would make navigating my neighborhood easier and less-stressful, like it was for my father and brother. After my epic fight with Nut, I began to experience the awe, fear, and respect of my perceived enemies now had toward me.

Fighting became my sport. This extra curricular activity became something I engaged to raise my self-confidence. Doing so would earn me a "rep" like my brother. I also didn't want to be physically accosted on a daily basis. 8th grade represents my acceleration into the abyss of violence and emotional malformation. I knew I had to prepare for the next level of urban gladiator training - high school.

Trauma Wars

From a broad view, trauma represents the significant experiences and shifts in a person's life that become turning points. These turning points would likely not have happened if the initial traumatic event did not take place. Aside from the bullying, poverty and violence, also being a light-skinned, Black male in the hood was a turning point for me. I experienced colorism (also called shadism). These are forms of hierarchical valuations of Black skin tones within the Black community. Specifically, light-skinned males were considered "soft" or non-threatening because their skin tone resembled whiteness. Colorism fuels discord between varying shades of Black folks due to past and present valuation systems of racial oppression. For no other reason than my being a very light-skinned Black male, I experienced a critical shift that made my life even more traumatic.

Ninth grade represented a social and personal quantum leap. By the time I entered high school I began to pierce through the social awkwardness that plagued me. I willed myself to do things that required interacting with other kids my age. I figured out that if I didn't allow guys to disrespect or punk me - especially in front of others - I could be very sociable. In high school, this social comfortability allowed me to display my humorous side.

My humor resonated well with girls my age. I became chronically distracted by attention from the opposite sex. Soon I would be consumed by promiscuity. Where I once was preparing myself to battle older boys and establish a "rep" for myself, I didn't prepare for the deluge of girls seeking my attention and affection because of my light skin and "good" hair *inter alia*.

Ill prepared, I jumped head first into the world of emotionless, exploratory, and meaningless sex with multiple partners. Between my comedic wit and self-confidence as a fighter, I was an attractive light-skinned beau who also could provide a protective element for the girls I dealt with. I started getting envious looks from guys from all grades. They were vexed by the attention I was receiving that they weren't. As a result, I got into a few physical altercations in the back hallways of West Side High

School. Nothing serious, but fights nonetheless. I became self-conscious about my light-skin and felt the urgent need to appear as a "roughneck." The feeling of having to stand-out from my light-skin peers stained my consciousness. I had to become ferocious and feared to ensure I didn't have the soft persona of other light-skinned brothers.

Colorism came into play during one fight where my brother made an appearance. Rah was a senior at West Side High School when I was a freshman. Someone alerted him that his little brother was fighting. The 11th grader I fought was a "come-up" - someone trying to establish a rep for himself by picking a fight so he can get some street cred. He wrongly thought I would be a sweet and easy victory just because I was a freshman, and light-skinned.

The fight had just ended and I handled the guy easily. At the same time my brother and his road-dog (Wu) violently burst through the doors of the hallway where the fight took place. Upon seeing me, they asked if I was aight. I responded "Hell, yeah!"- very proudly. I gave my brother a brief summary and they left quickly.

Instinctually, because they left so abruptly I felt the need to follow them. When I caught them on another floor of the school, they had accosted the 11th grader I just fought. My brother and Wu began whooping his ass, right in the middle of the hallway, brazenly laying down a barrage of punches to the guy's face and skull. People just watched, as if it was a normal school activity.

My brother and Wu ceased their battering and mixed in the crowd before the teachers and staff responded to the ruckus. As we all dispersed, I heard two girls talking about the commotion that just went down. One said to the other, "I think they fucked him up because he was trying to bully Rah's little brother, a freshman." Hearing their words made me feel so low and disrespected. My brother's actions lessened my rep. Not good! Part of me loved my brother for his actions and a part of me thought he did it because he had a penchant for violence and was worried about his rep. Again, my misperceptions. I should just have embraced it as the former.

I found him in the cafeteria and asked, "That's fucked up! Why fuck him up when I already did it?"

He looked at me with the coldest gaze I ever received from him and responded, "Because you didn't! He ain't got no scars, no blood on him. You didn't advertise your work. That's what you gotta do if you want respect around here."

I was so confused by my brother's statement. "What did I miss?" I thought to myself. The guy conceded and ran in retreat from my attack. I thought that you only reciprocated the ferocity that was leveled at you. I clearly won the fight. But even in the midst of a war time victory, I was learning some life and death urban survival warfare tactics on the fly. It was truly a "trial by fire" for me with a magnitude of consequences I still didn't fully understand.

I was moving through hostile territory without a proper mission briefing. Everyone essentially became an enemy because I felt unaware of *who* my enemy was and, more importantly, *why* they were my enemy. Neither did I know what questions to ask nor did I have a blueprint for how to be thoroughly and fearfully respected in order to advance through the hood. High school was no longer a place for academic training and enrichment. It became a training center for social survival skills.

Months later, toward the end of my freshman year, a senior stole me (sucker-punched) me for no reason. I was confused as to why. I couldn't retaliate because I was dazed. He darted-off quickly. My brother told me later that seniors will randomly single-out an underclassman for a sucker punch because they are leaving school for good. However, this was not one of those random occasions. This senior was someone my brother once beat-up so he sought his revenge on me. This was my wake-up call. I would not let this go. *I could not let this go!* My brother knew where the guy lived and said he would deal with him.

"No! I'mma handle it" I told my brother emphatically.

"You know ol' boy stays strapped (carries a gun) every now and then, right?" he said casually. Whoa! I totally didn't know that, but I replied coolly and confidently, "Yeah, I know. But if it's not in his hands when I get him, so what?"

This was new terrain for me. I didn't know I was built like that and never even thought of challenging a guy who carries a gun. I had heard tales in the hood about gangsta' shit like that. So I just repeated it to my brother because I thought that's what needed to be said by me in order for him to allow me to handle my own wartime affairs. I walked away anxiously thinking, "Damn! That mother fucker be packin'?" Interestingly, I was not scared and I was actually plotting my revenge against a person known to carry guns. I had never been in a situation that involved gunplay. I'd heard about it and witnessed it but I never, ever, touched a gun for violent purposes. I saw a guy get shot not too far from my house, and heard that he died from it when I was 11. That's the closest I'd been to gun violence up to that point. I was in violent virgin territory.

At this point in my young life, the scope of aggression and violence I engaged in was either menacingly snarling, throwing "bass" (raising your voice) at someone, or outright fist fighting. Weaponized violence was of utmost seriousness. And because of the level of trauma and dysfunctionality I was already immersed in, I wasn't even fearful about the high potential for fatal consequences. I wasn't concerned about getting shot, killed, shooting or killing him or hurting any innocent bystanders. My mindset was steadily and relentlessly moving towards a criminal frame of mind.

Bad Boy

No child is born bad... is a truth that is systemically not seen in or applied to Black children in American juridical, social, educational, and penal practices or institutions. There are appalling historical and present day inequities and disparate racial realities deeply embedded into the fabric of American Black life. They are emblematic of the necessity for social justice organizations and movements safeguarding and fighting for the irrefutable fact that "Black Lives Matter" equally as other lives.

I'm compelled to illustrate how the socio-political factors and pressures that are the result of systemic inequality or racism substantially contribute to the creation of the violent juvenile-offender, otherwise known as the "bad kid."

During the summer after 9th grade I had, at least, three girlfriends and three possibles (girls who were putting up some resistance to my advancements but were interested in my attempts to begin a sexual relationship). Two of the girlfriends went to West Side High School with me and the others went to Barringer High School, also in Newark. The three possibles lived in various areas around, near or in Newark. I became very sexually active at this point. And not just because of juvenile carnal exploration, sexual curiosity or hormones. I did so purely from a misogynistic place that accompanied my new hyper-masculine identity.

I wanted my sexual achievements to be known and the multiple conquests to be acknowledged. The achievements were part of the persona I wanted to project publicly. This behavior was meant to signal my manliness. It also boasted my courage to boldly violate the territories of other boys in pursuit of their girls. These feats are what rewards a socially and emotionally dysfunctional persona sunken in such a broken environment. These environmental factors cultivate the worst human potential so exactly, that they have been the principal point of analyses in Black Renaissance literature.

Writers, such as Ralph Ellison and James Baldwin wrote about how the socio-political pressures placed on Black people from anti-Black racist systems of oppression drove them, in part, toward their unseemly ways. Violence, drug use, criminality, and religion became avenues to cope with the horrible realities of racialized oppression.

Ultimately, my sexist and violent actions masked my insecurities, my pain, my inner-hurt and confusion. Like so many young men, I felt compelled to adopt a hyper-masculinity identity. I became entrenched with the psyche so many Black males in poor, dysfunctional communities possessed. This attitude made its way into my young mind and firmly rooted itself. With a toxic attitude, I objectified the young girls in my school. Many of them were promiscuous for their own traumatic reasons, allowing themselves to be used as sexual objects. Their low esteem allowed me to amplify my prowess as a means of collecting some status points to strengthen my reputation.

I began subscribing to the belief that my feelings mattered above anything and anyone else's. I didn't know it then but by adopting a hyper-masculine identity I would become a misogynist, homophobe, verbal and emotional abuser, and develop an antisocial personality. My freshman year was the blooming period for this new identity. That year I overcame any social condemnations of being a punk and was promoted to a reputation of someone who would "put in work." I faintly sensed fear in my male social counterparts whenever I'd come around them or when we met up at particular hangouts - neighborhood stores that had a few arcade games in them or the large porch of an abandoned building. I wouldn't resort to bullying a guy unless I was trying to provoke them into a confrontation because I thought they were a bully. I hated bullies! I was sure to challenge them. Most of the time I did this publicly without compunction.

The incident that solidified my rep as someone to be respected and feared involved my revenge on that gun-toting senior who stole me earlier that year. Not only was my "bad boy" rep set through it, but my belief in my emotional hardness and comfortability in wearing a hyper-masculine identity as a mask crystalized. The revenge I wanted on this guy obsessed me for weeks. That incident was brought up in random social settings as part of our "Hood

Tales "- conversation or gossip about events in the neighborhood. It was described as my beef with him by others, but I didn't see it that way. Through my young, social novice's eyes I got chumped by a gun-toting senior from across the park. But in precisely dysfunctional fashion, paradoxically, it was for those very reasons the situation was coined a beef. Remember, according to my brother I wasn't randomly selected as an easy mark. Unbeknownst to me, I was the middle-man between two individuals who had a rep for putting in work.

I began feeling the respect and fear of me from my peers from my willingness to participate in violent Hood warfare. They knew I was obsessed with exacting revenge on the senior because I didn't hide it. Being so open with it was a novice move on my part. Advertising my hostile intent would surely get back to him. Lucky for me, it gave me a stronger advantage. I would walk across the park looking for him not having the faintest clue of what I'd do if I saw him. I was moved only by my emotions. As weeks passed, my obsession waned because though I didn't catch up to him, I received info that he was still around. After realizing the futility of my search efforts, I decided to stop pursuing retribution and instead wait for its delivery. This was easier said than done, though. I was now dealing with weaponized violence - the kind that kills whether you intend it to or not. This possibility was ever on my mind, so much that it sculpted my mindset toward hostile readiness. Though my fixation on payback subsided in intensity, it never went away completely. Actually, it began manifesting itself through the constant, outward projection of aggressive behavior.

I displayed an air of anger as a mask because I was portraying both someone who I inherently wasn't and I was scared shitless about running into the senior when he could be armed and I wasn't. My thought was, "Until I can get a gun, why try to encounter him? Let me just wait until I can get a piece." Though my rep was at its height, I didn't want to become one of the brazenly ridiculous Hood Tales about individuals challenging someone who was packing heat while unarmed and subsequently dying.

Good fortune was on my side one day in early September, right before school started. I noticed the senior in Dr. Jay's sneaker store while I was in downtown Newark shopping for school clothes. He was so focused on talking with the store's attendant about purchasing a pair of Fila sneakers that he never spotted me. I casually walked behind the adjacent clothes rack to conceal myself and gain a clearer look to confirm it was him. "God dammit, that's that motherfucker," I silently exclaimed to myself. The realization held for me both nervousness and excitement. I smoothly and unnoticeably exited the store. As soon as the outside air struck my nostrils, I thought, "What the fuck do I do now?" I resolved myself not to panic and nonchalantly walked away from the store. I then turned into the first alley. That day, I had no bags to worry about securing in my waistband. "I'm getting mine's from this motherfucker today," I cheerfully thought to myself.

I remained happy about the opportunity to get payback on this dude despite the grim reality that had me wondering, "What if he's packing a gun?" As soon as that thought materialized, my eyes looked down and noticed a metal pipe of a good weight nearby. I knew it could induce the blunt force trauma I was going for and it had an ergonomically correct handle at which to grip it. Though I couldn't choose any of the weapons from my personal armory, this pipe and the element of surprise was enough to justify an assault on this dude (whether he had a gun or not). I just needed to wait until he walked out of the store. I picked up the short-sized pipe and placed it in my right front pocket and pulled my shirt over the end to conceal it. I positioned my back at the corner facing Dr. Jay's so I could see the traffic in and out of the store. There were crowds of people walking on the streets or waiting for the bus. This could help or hurt my advantage, I sized up internally.

I waited 15 minutes for him to exit the store. During that time I visualized different scenarios of how to "run down" on him. I eventually quelled all the feelings and plans of how to attack this guy and settled on being spontaneous and ferocious. The senior exited the store and turned toward my direction, walking closest to the curb of the sidewalk. I was on the same sidewalk but closer to the buildings. I walked with a crowd of people in the direction toward him. He couldn't see me and I walked right past him. I turned around and followed him, still undetected.

There were still a lot of people in the fray. "Don't rush it; don't blow it, Damon," I admonished myself. The senior walked toward the end of the block and turned into the next alleyway. I thought to myself, "Maybe this is a sign to get him later. He probably spotted me," I dispiritedly said to myself. I tracked him a bit more and since he was walking coolly with bags in his hands, unworried, I might still have my chance. I secured the pipe in my hand and speedily tip-toed towards him, chanting to myself, "I got the drop on this motherfuckerrrrrr!"

My heart raced and thumped inside my chest as I closed in on striking distance. I crept closer and he still didn't suspect a thing. If he had a gun, though, I was still vulnerable. I had to go through with this. I entered the strike zone and landed a solid blow to the back of his head. It wasn't 100% but had power behind it! I wasn't trying to murder him but I wanted him to know it was me to make this revenge mission count.

The senior dazedly fell down, semi-conscious, as if a boxer dropped by a hard uppercut punch. He hit the ground hard and rolled on his back. His eyes were looking off into nowhere, they were open but he wasn't seeing anything because his brains were scrambled. There was no need to hit him again.

The senior was defenseless. Now I needed to send a message to him and others like him. I stood over him, cocky as fuck, and said, "Remember me?" He mumbled something incoherent as he stretched his hands up to me. After a second or two in this state of incoherency, his eyes fixed on me in a way that reflected that he was both gaining some coherence and memory of me.

I then thwacked his knee with all my might and felt something crack in it. This blow woke him up but also placed him in agonizing and writhing pain. I dragged him behind some big metal dumpsters to shield us from passersby. My mental clock is counting down and I'm anxiously telling myself,

"This shit shouldn't last no more than 2 minutes, Damon." He began squealing so loudly from both the pain of the blows and also trying to get noticed by someone or to receive help, that I put my hand over his mouth. I threw some hard punches to his face that were escorted with some harsh words. I was feeling myself; enjoying the power of violence and the empowering feeling of revenge. "Where's your gun now, motherfucker," I mockingly asked him.

He was teetering on unconsciousness by this time and his body was near-lifeless. I hit him with rage-fueled savageness. It was time to bring my retribution to an end. I hurt him badly, the kind of bad that gives a person a permanent limp or scar. As I was turning to leave him there victimized and behind the dumpster, something told me to go back. I turned, grabbed him, and reached under the back of his shirt into the waistband of his pants. Voilà! There it was - his gun! "Jackpot!" I remember saying to myself.

My sudden decision to check for a gun came from some movements he made during the attack that didn't register with me at that moment. The senior was cognizant enough during the assault to keep his back to the ground. During some non-threatening instances, he did try to extend his hand around his back. I initially thought he was spasming from the hurting I put on him but my intuition stopped me and directed me exactly to what my inner eyes needed me to see. I grabbed the handle of his gun and appraised it very quickly. It was a 32. caliber automatic pistol with a six inch barrel. I remember feeling a cascading rush of mixed emotions and thoughts as I gripped the gun. "My gun!" I said to myself. This torrent of sensation overwhelmed me because in the deep recesses of my fifteen year old child psyche I knew I wasn't prepared for the responsibility that came with carrying a gun. Every molecule of my being knew it was wrong. But the dysfunctional reasoning I began subscribing to hijacked my childhood innocence and desire to be a "good kid." Unfortunately, what I thought was a serendipitous discovery that would ultimately put me on gangsta level status in the Hood was actually the second to last stage of my becoming a violent, juvenile offender. I was deep into the makings of a "bad kid."

Out of Control

I entered 10th grade with a made-up mind on two points: 1) I had no intention of applying myself in my studies and 2) I had no fear of carrying a gun to class. The gun - my gun - was proof of payment for my Hood credentials and street rep. I unknowingly bartered my future prospects in life in exchange for a fleeting experience of fame and worthless notoriety. This social recognition would become a self-destructive, negative loop. I knew I didn't want a career as a thug or gansta, but the violence and toxic environment totally gutted me of any ability to withstand negative peer-pressure. Wanting to feel, know and display my self-worth became more important than planning for a better life. As a result, the more I played the part of a callous, uncaring tough Newark kid, the more I was internally encouraged and swayed to live him out in real life. I began wearing the signature Hip Hop-style clothing that signaled I was "down by law" and street certified. I was also willing, and even seeking, to defend my prized attired social-fashioned statements in any kind of encounter.

That year I wore the B-boy street uniforms - Kangol hats, shelled-toed Adidas, Izod shirts and Lee jeans or Lee jean jackets, Cazal glasses and belt-buckles. My ears kept a pair of Sony Walkman headphones on them while playing the booming, mind-numbing tracks of Run DMC, Grandmaster Flash and the Furious Five, Eric B. and Rakim, and LL Kool J. This media form became my inspiration and knowledge source. Hip Hop was the model of how I would live because the lyrics empowered me through its sense of familiarity with my life experiences. It gave purpose to a very confused, hurt and impressionable kid who was full of potential. From my perspective, I was drowning in an environment that lacked opportunities to cultivate that potential. My disobedience rose to an outright performance of serious defiance and rebelliousness, mostly evidenced through risky activities and self-harm.

My love affair with Hip-Hop steadily increased while I was losing any desire to apply myself academically. I went to school just to participate in the fashion exhibitions and gossip in the cafeteria, hallways, bathrooms and occasional classes. Positive life lessons were far from being learned. School was now the place to get my fill of social capital by wearing the latest $100 Jordans, stylish name brand glasses, Wallabies (shoes), or being asked questions about a fight or beef I had.

Imagine a bad kid increasing his promiscuity and criminality. My behaviors had intensified considerably. The promiscuity demanded that I court and woo girls wherever I went. Doing so would increase my contact with other violent young men in their territories. These encounters inevitably escalated my involvement in criminality because most of them resulted in taking the spoils from the victims of the violence. Procuring people's Hip-Hop statements was rationalized to justify the adage, "To the victor goes the spoils." Money was always the primary motivation for these actions but there was a social currency earned from it too.

I correlated my self-worth to my ability to exercise domination over others. Like so many young Black boys and men, I felt a need for and sought self- and social-approval. It was such a great need that it gnawed into my sense of communal and cooperative engagement. It made my mindset selfish and intensely rugged. Unfortunately, this oppressive, dog-eat-dog mentality that pervades impoverished communities creates a precarious interpersonal social dynamic. The Hood is where the very person that could become your bestie (best friend) and road-dog could also become your mortal enemy or vic (victim). This dynamic formed, and continues to form, a distrusting and deep-rooted fear of people in my community.

These concepts were further compounded by the racialized and harassing police presence and experiences I experienced as a young kid. I felt like I had to act like a rebellious, dangerous man. Despite being a kid, I was approached by law enforcement and treated by them and other authoritative figures as an adult. Even before my waywardness began, my encounters with police had been early "stop and frisk" situations. As 10 and 12 year old kids we knew not to travel in packs to the park or recreational events. Doing so would have us get "run down on" by the undercovers or narcos. We were conditioned to feel disempowered by officials and authorities at a very early age. History documents this period that many of us Black children were "left behind" by a school system that was not equipped, or perhaps didn't care, to help us adequately prepare ourselves to successfully compete and excel socially.

During these times I was careful not to showcase my gun. I only occasionally brought it to school because my street wisdom compelled me not to diminish the source of fear and respect I obtained from my hand skills (fighting). My piece was more of an insurance policy when things got "too thick." I fell in love with fighting and it became my first conflict resolution option.

Guns became a common weapon of choice in the Hood because of the explosion of drugs in our communities. The money made from dealing drugs raised Hood recognition and reputation even higher. Dealers wore fancy clothes and jewelry. They drove shiny cars, too. Neither did I admire nor was I impressed by the dealers in the Hood, though. I honestly believed that most of them were soft. Because I wasn't socialized in the drug life, I wasn't greatly influenced by its activity.

My area of town hadn't been inundated by dealers because there were a lot of "stick-up" boys in it. I'd see them walk up to dealers and strong arm them (rob them without a gun or knife). So my socialization was one of being brazen and "bad' enough to take what you want, from anybody you want. In retrospect, I was so traumatized by the violence in my community that I never imagined I could leave or use other socially unacceptable activities (like drug dealing) to acquire money in which to facilitate an eventual exit. I had been so psychologically defeated to the point that I couldn't visualize myself existing outside a space of powerlessness and dysfunction. Visiting my girlfriends and fighting the boys in their Hood occupied my entire sophomore year. Some of these beefs resulted in alliances, truces or continued warfare "on sight."

Through all of this, I evaded the scrutiny and concern of my parents by holding down a job here and there at a grocery store or fast-food restaurant. Although my academic initiative waned, school was easy to keep from being a concern because all I had to do was attend and do the bare minimum and to pass. Some years later I'd have conversations with my mom about this period in my life. She would acknowledge that she suspected something was going on but just attributed it to my transition from one stage of development into another. She knew it was too late when she finally understood what was happening. By then I learned how to cover my tracks, tell a convincing lie, or put on a good act to ensure she wasn't seeing what she was actually seeing in her son.

In all fairness to my mother, she couldn't shield me from the hard truths of the world. She needed to watch over my younger sisters, too. This allowed me to finesse past my parent's authority. They weren't overly concerned by the increase in my fighting because it was something young men and young women ultimately had to experience and learn from in the Hood.

My life seriously began to really unravel when I started getting invitations for alliances and friendships from guys outside of my Hood. I became recognized as a *thorough motherfucker.* This heightened status, bestowed upon me by those who could have been formidable enemies, sent my ego into overdrive. The popularity overrode my senses and restructured my mind, my thoughts. The bad kid in me was given the green light to determine my future. What a terrible choice I made. Psychoanalytically speaking, the ego is "the part of the mind that mediates between the conscious and the unconscious and is responsible for reality testing and a sense of personal identity," see (https://www.bing.com/search?q=define+ego&form=DCTRQR Microsoft Bing, Definition of the Ego). Thus, when I received the attention of other gun-toting thugs with a rep (a personal identity) who saw me as someone who would reliably put in work while watching their backs, squeeze the hammer when necessary, give out fair ones, accept them on sight, and win them - my soul was sold to the streets (by my ego).

I'd given myself over to the losing side for nothing. All I got was a fleeting socio-emotional motivated pleasure experience. When I think of this period in my life, I can't help but think of it as a metaphor for the wages of sin. A story that comes to mind is the imaginary tale of Dr. Faustus. "A man makes a deal with the devil: in exchange for his body and soul, the man is to receive supernatural power and pleasures for 24 years. The devil agrees to the trade, and Dr. Faustus enjoys the pleasures of sin for a season, but his doom is sealed. At the end of 24 years, Faustus attempts to thwart the devil's plans, but he meets a frightful demise, nonetheless," see (https://www.gotquestions.org/sell-soul-devil.html Selling your soul to the Devil, Dr. Faustus). I sold my soul; I no longer found goodness attractive.

My rep rang bells and extended outside my own Hood as someone "not to fuck wit" but such a rep is a double-edged sword. It brings both offers of alliances and violently senseless beefs. In a normal civilized and equitable society, I should have had a singular anxiety about having an exciting summer of amusement parks and going to the beach with friends as a sophomore in High School. I should have been concerned about getting fun before I started college. Instead, I was dreading being killed for wearing nice clothes or jewelry that others placed more value on than my life. I should have had anxiety about the increasing numbers of female sexual conquests and my rep as a Mack or Ladies Man. My puerile heart, mind and soul were ravaged beyond anything that could be considered a normal childhood experience.

Literally Dodging Bullets

One day I was passing through Central Avenue. I happened to be strapped. A guy named Khaleef, who had just come home from a juvenile reformatory bid for shooting someone, was sitting on a porch with about three other guys. I knew all of them from elementary and middle school and they knew me. I thought nothing about these guys hanging on the porch in their Hood. As I walked by, one of them greeted me, "What's up with you, *Damien*? (one of my aliases)"

"Nothing up with me, Has (short for Hassan). What's up with you?" I quickly replied as I kept stepping. Before Has could even respond, Khaleef calmly announced, "Damien, if you know what's good for you, you betta not come through here again."

I stopped in my tracks a very short distance away from the porch and pivoted an about-face to look right at him. My immediate, unwavering pivot was necessary. I had girls I was courting in this Hood and unfettered access was not just convenient but mandatory. Although I was confused and surprised by the unsolicited slight, I didn't have time to be scared or inquisitive about his motives, which I was prone to doing. Facing him, I gestured both my hands in a questioning manner as I disrespectfully intonated, "Let's act like I don't know what's good for me."

At the very moment of this pronouncement, everyone on the porch instantaneously stood up on alert, as if an emergency bell had set off. Has promptly tried to be a peacemaker and neutralize the situation by saying, "Go ahead, Damien, just keep walking. That ain't about nothing."

But Khaleef, wanting to further escalate it, hollered in a mocking tone, "Yeah, go ahead Damien, before you get some hot shit put in you." I probingly thought to myself, "How the fuck did this shit happen? I'm just trying to get to north Newark and this motherfucker's talking about shooting me!"

I suddenly became enraged and my adrenaline quickly soared beyond this earth. You don't have to be from the Hood to know that he clearly meant putting a bullet in me - shooting me for walking through his Hood. A lightning bolt of fear had in fact accompanied my rage, too. "What to do now?" I rapidly thought to myself. I couldn't dismiss his threat. It seemed like an eternity as I thought through my options in response to Khaleef's warning.

But the doubts lasted only a split second.

I don't remember making any specific decision. I just reached underneath the front of my shirt and whipped out my gun. With pure confidence, I said, "Hot shit from somethin' like this?"

In my short life, I learned that once you pull out (show your weapon) you better use it or else people will think you're bluffing. You had to show your willingness to be bloodthirsty and serious about carrying out your violent resolve. I was now locked in on displaying my willingness to engage in a shootout with these guys.

All at once they scattered by either jumping off the porch and running away or bolted inside the door to the building.

Hands up, but not evacuating from the porch, Has yelled emphatically, "Nah, Damien!"

He didn't have to run from me. He knew we had no beef. Khaleef, though, didn't run like the others. "This dude was crazy, stupid or thought I was soft since I was light-skinned," I thought.

Has walked in front of Khaleef; shielding him, as he spoke pleadingly to me. My internal clock is ticking, my heart is racing. In an adrenaline fueled state of mind, I'm telling myself to make a decision. I don't know where the other guys ran to, or what they'll bring back.

"Move, Has!" I ordered, as I'm swiveling my head looking at all my vulnerable and exposed points. Has, now noticeably shaking, says, "Come on, Damien. Just let it go. He just came home, man."

Has was insinuating in simple terms that Khaleef didn't know any better. He was unaware of who's who and the standings in the Hood because he had been locked-up. Or, he could have implied that Khaleef's mindset is still in jail-mode and that he's just being aggressive without thinking. I really didn't try to process whatever that actually meant. In fact, it reminded me that this dude had no problem with pulling the trigger at someone.

After thinking about this, I unhesitatingly shot into the floor of the porch, inches away from Khaleef's foot. I hostilely stated, "I shoot, too, mothafucka! Let this dummy know who I am, Has."

I looked both ways and speedily continued the way I came while looking back at them. Khaleef hurried into the hallway. Has walked to the porch railing, grabbed it with both hands leaning on outstretched arms, and just shook his head in disbelief. I knew what was going on in his mind. It wasn't just personal relief about not getting shot; he knew this had some future implications that would undoubtedly involve some gun play.

Gossip travels fast in the Hood. When I got back to my Hood on 14th Avenue some hours later, I went by some of the hangout spots. The word was out! Damien shot at Khaleef. I also found out that Khaleef came looking for me. That wasn't a surprise to me, him showing up by himself was. That immediately signaled that Has and the other dudes on the porch might not want any parts of our beef.

I hastily went to Central Avenue, looking for Has. I knew where he lived and made a bee-line there to get intel on Khaleef. Some of the spontaneous actions I engaged in were precipitated by what I heard a Hood gangsta should do in certain situations. All of the moves were highly impulsive decisions and actions.

So I walked into Has' apartment building and went to the second floor. I knocked on his door with one hand, while gripping the gun behind my leg with the other. Has' sister, who I knew socially, opened the door. As soon as she saw me, her countenance signaled awareness of something unusual. It wasn't an alarm but she knew I never came to see her brother before.

"Hey, Damien!" She warmly greeted me.

"Wassup, Cent (short for Cynthia). "Has, here?"

"Hasss!!" she yelled loudly toward the back of the apartment as she seductively, but effortlessly, strutted her big shapely hips away from the door.

"Damn! Milk does a body good, huh, Cent?" I jokingly blurted out to her, as I was trying to get a feel for her interest in me while I followed closely behind her into the apartment living room. Immediately after she left my eyesight, Has appeared in the doorway of the living room. As soon as he saw me, he peacefully said, "Damien, that's between you and him."

The rules of the streets teach us to not take people's word at face value. But as there are exceptions to each rule, I believed this moment to be an exception. And I took Has at his word. I simply replied to him, "Enuff said, Has. We cool. But your man came looking for me just now. I'mma handle that. You know what I'm saying?"

Has, looking at me droopily, says, "Whatever, Dame. That's between y'all." I raised my hand to meet his gesture for "The Pound" - one dap (handshake) up and down and one to close out - I left and he closed the door.

There was so much respect and fear granted to those with a gun-toting Hood identity. I was glad for that status because I had unfettered access to the Hood and its girls. The drug-dealing hustlers were there, too, but dealing didn't guarantee you respect and fear. I tried hustling but it just wasn't my thing. It made me feel too vulnerable. It was a pressure-filled and stressful occupation. Dealers were easy targets for the robbers. Hell, when I needed quick cash I'd act as if I was trying to cop some drugs. And because they were so eager and under pressure to sell their drugs, I'd whip out the gun and take their money and drugs.

I wanted to pursue a social role that required applying pressure, not one you had to receive pressure from. I was so uninformed, so lost. The average drug dealer wasn't an easy victim, they packed heat or had a squad with them. But I chose the Hood thug role and it required me to see myself as the apex black market actor. So I began living out that role. Usually, when I was able to catch a dealer off guard, I'd keep the money and jewelry and give the drugs away to people I was tight with. I didn't know it then but that gesture earned me favors in the form of information.

A week or two before entering the 11th grade, on a warm, sunny day, I walked outside of a Bodega about a block away from my home. I had a box of Little Debbie Oatmeal Crème pies, a bag of barbecue Bon-Ton potato chips, and a Nehi orange soda.

Pow! A shot rang out. I kneeled down a little, looking in the direction I thought the bullet came from. It was from my center-right side. The bullet smashed into the wooden frame of the Bodega's door, about 6 inches near my face. Had it hit me, the force would have been life-ending. Wood splinters bounced off my face from the bullet's impact. People began to duck and scatter.

Pow! A second shot rang out but I couldn't tell what was hit. I was already looking to my right, across the street. As people were ducking and screaming in front of the Bodega, I saw Khaleef across the street. He was crouched down and pointing his gun in my direction.

I never dropped my snacks and was high from smoking weed blunts. I didn't get nervous. By this point in my life I had been around gunshots before but this was different. These shots were aimed at me. Strangely, I maintained my composure and did not panic while under live fire. After spotting him, my eyes locked on him. A quick thought of stepping back into the Bodega entered my mind but I quickly disregarded the notion. "Don't box yourself in Dame," I thought to myself. I can't go back into the store and I'm not running from him because I'd be giving him my back to shoot.

Pow! He fires a third shot at me. It hits the ground between two parked cars, one of which I'm behind. I'm still crouching down and peering at him through the parked car window. He sees me looking at him. Then he takes his eyes off me and fixes them on his gun. "Something's up with his gun," I told myself, as I dropped my snacks and began untying my sweatpants. They had an inside pocket where I kept my shooter. I decided to lure him towards me.

This was a life or death stakes game. My courage (a courage I never knew was in me and one that should have been directed towards a positive end) allowed me to keep my wits. I had hoped to make him think he had me without a gun and become bold enough to run down on me. Whatever was going on with his gun was far better for me. Still kneeling, I scurried to the back of the car and saw Khaleef crouching down, too. "Fuck it!," I said, pumping myself up.

Too much time had lapsed without any movement for a guy with the advantage of surprise - and a gun. I rose up, and came out from behind the car, totally exposed myself and pointed my gun at Khaleef. I had him dead-to-right. The look in his eyes even confirmed he was got. The drop I had on him was so clear and unobstructed that I didn't have to cross the street.

"Don't kill him," I said to myself before I shot him once in the thigh. When he turned to run, dropping his gun and grimacing in pain, I gave him another one in the back left shoulder. As I was firing at him, I yelled, "What's up now, bitch! Still gonna put some hot shit in me?" He painfully ran from the scene, despite his wounds. I did an about-face and went my own way as casually as one could saunter away from shooting someone.

Sad to say, I wasn't scared of the police coming to arrest me. There were two major reasons. First, as long as it wasn't a murder both the police and most individuals in the Hood could care less what happened, and didn't want to get involved. Second, I knew Khaleef was from the breed of dudes that would keep the beef in the street and not report it to the cops. I went home, changed clothes and hid the gun. I made a couple of phone calls to meet up with some people later that day but never mentioned to anyone what took place.

When I met up with some of my dudes, I found a reason for us to walk through where the shooting took place. I donned a hat and shades as we approached the Bodega. It was five to six hours later with no signs of cops or crowds.

We then headed to a hangout spot of ours nearby. It was a 24-hour store with video games that sold chicken wings and sandwiches. We went in and it was crowded. We ordered some wings and watched people play arcade games but I was really there to ear-hustle for news. About 15-minutes after we got there, a group of loud talking kids charged-in arguing about how many shots were fired. Everybody in the store got silent and all eyes and ears were on their every word.

The kids were giving their version of the shootout. “Some Spanish guy shot Khaleef from Central Avenue today,” one kid recounted. As I listened more, a sense of relief overcame me because the word on the street was different than what actually happened - and it wasn’t me doing the shooting.

“Is he dead,” a voice inquired. “Nah, he good. We just seen him get in a car with his peeps,” the other voice returned. Feeling relieved about no police involvement and Khaleef not dying from his gunshots, I didn’t need any fanfare about my gunplay by civilians. The individuals who needed to know who really shot Khaleef would certainly find out. The

Hood news and grapevine system just worked like that.

About two weeks after the shooting I received word from Khaleef. Initially, I had heard that Cent came looking for me. I immediately knew that whatever she wanted involved the bang-out with Khaleef. My curiosity took over and I had to see what she wanted - ASAP! I went to her apartment building on full alert, carrying my gun cocked and loaded in my right hand. The hallway lights were out and the door was open, and I masked my fear with a brazen attitude by walking hard and loudly up the stairs. I knocked on the door and Has opened it. It looked like he saw a ghost. His mouth was opened and his eyes were wide as can be. I put him at ease quickly.

I didn't want him to panic and then do something that would make me have to respond violently. So with a smile on my face and a friendly tone I said to him, "We aight, right?" In a relaxed and relieved state, he smilingly said, "Always!" We dapped and hugged. He let me in the apartment and I sat down in the living room. I told him Cent came looking for me and I wanted to know why. He responded, "Khaleef's sister gave her a message for you."

As me and Has sat in the living room, Cent peeked her head through the doorway, and with a smirk on her face, said, "Hey, light-skin! Let's talk in my bedroom." Certain encounters in our lives, despite how uneventful or impactful they may seem or feel at the time, can have an everlasting effect on us - for good or bad. My encounter with Cent that day is a moment in my life in which the seeds of critical and honest self-appraising were sown. I went into her bedroom with both an expectation of getting a message from someone trying to kill me, which would have eased my anxiety-ridden state of mind, and hopes I'd get into her panties.

Get this visual of Cent: she was the 1985 version of Beyonce' with a Megan Da Stallion body! My thoughts about her were uncontrollable. But Cent, to my surprise, was 22-years old. I was only 16. I entered her bedroom and it was pristinely decked out in pink. She had a desk in her bedroom that was laden with college books, a typewriter and composition notebooks. This definitely told me she was older than me. I was intimidated but I knew I had to dial-down my childish gestures, letting her know I was interested. Though she was outta my league (I thought) and everything about her bedroom and how it was arranged loudly acknowledged that fact. But my ego and sexual desire was stronger than my self-restraint. I had resolved myself to wait for an opportunity to come at her with some of my "How's my Chances?" rap.

Distracted, I almost forgot about her having information from a guy trying to kill me. I came back to reality, and out of the daydream of me smashing Cent on her bed, upon hearing, "Damon! You listening to me? Do I have your attention? Or you just wanna keep staring at my butt," she annoyingly announced. "Huh," I goofily replied.

As soon as we hit her bedroom, Cent closed the door and did an about-face towards me with her hands still clutching the door knob. She spews out a litany of inquiries and opinions, such as, "Do you wanna die out here in these streets? You can be anything you wanna be Damon because I heard how smart you are in school but you don't apply yourself or you just don't go at all. I got girl cousins that know you and go to West Side with you. Most of the people that know you and grew up around the way with you all say you're heading down a fucked-up road. You can't see it - or maybe you don't wanna see it - but the path you're on now, you'll be dead or in jail in less than a year. This shit you brothers out here doin' to each other is for NOTHINGGG! Makes me sick!"

I was stunned and I didn't want to address her interrogation. Deep down I just couldn't. I felt powerless on every level of being. I feebly replied, "I got a lot going on right now that you wouldn't understand."

Cent quickly shot back, "I understand more than your young ass do and what you think I know. See, all that glitters ain't gold, Damon. We don't know what's going on behind closed doors to people's lives and homes. You're suffering from the 'Grass is greener next door" complex. You think nobody has it worse than you. Wrong! A lot of people, including me, ain't carrying guns and hurting others because we got abused or victimized." Cent was on a high of emotional expressiveness and her eyes even welled with tears. She cared about me yet we barely knew one another. On the other hand, all I could do is think to myself, "Whoa! Cent is sexy, smart, *and* has goals in life."

Looking back on my encounter with Cent, this was my crisis intervention. Some of what she said actually began to anchor into my thoughts. She gave me too much stuff to think about, even what I didn't want to think about.

I decided to divert the conversation and sternly interjected, "So what about Khaleef?" Sensing my frustration, Cent humbly responded, "I didn't want to get in the middle of this, but since Khaleef's sister is my friend, and she doesn't know you, I told her I'd give you the message if it was peaceful. So I'm telling you this: Khaleef says he don't want no problems. He said you got that. You ain't got to worry about him if you see him." While listening to her my face had twisted-up so clearly in disbelief, that Cent grabbed my arm softly and said, "I think I believe him."

"Why?" I said hardheartedly.

"Because Khaleef ain't who everybody thinks he is," she firmly snapped. "He's fucking scared as hell of you. He hasn't stopped crying about him almost dying since you shot him," she said with exasperation.

Still doubtful about his peace offer, I told Cent to send this message: "I accept it. But if he gives me any bad looks I don't like, I'm firing off, period." I was about to leave but Cent told me to stay. She wanted me to hear the phone conversation between her and Khaleef's sister. They were on the phone for 20 minutes, while I just laid on Cent's bed or messed around in her things as she occasionally chided to me, "Red-boy leave my stuff alone." I wasn't ear-hustling on their phone call because I was enamored with the décor of Cent's bedroom and she sporadically included me into the conversation. I felt as though I was being sized up, tested by her. They were talking about me both indirectly and directly. I was accustomed to dealing with teenage girls, so my time with Cent, an older and much focused female, was a first for me. But I didn't panic; I maintained my poise and just went with my gut. And it was telling me that I should listen to Cent the same way I did to the so-called Hood icons.

After her phone call ended, Cent plopped down beside me on the bed. Bumping all her beautiful Black woman thickness on top of me first and then sliding down next to me. I couldn't disguise the excitement molded on my face. "Don't get any ideas horny man, let's just chill out, talk, smoke some bud or whatever," she said resolutely. And that's what we did 'til the morning came. From that day, Cent and I either talked on the phone every day or hung out in her bedroom or at a food spot. Our time together, though, came to an end in December 1985. She was going to another state to start college that Spring semester of 1986. During these weeks with Cent had me experience some good advice, life skills and how to plan.

My hoodlum activities ceased considerably though my school performance remained the same (I barely got by). More importantly, I began thinking about my future and what I wanted to do. Cent was a light that helped me begin to find the "me" that had been lost within for some time. Nevertheless, I was still trapped inside hostile terrain and had to be mindful that the streets don't care about a person's change of heart. I had open and on-sight beefs I had to stay aware of 24-7.

Warning Signs Everywhere

During this same time in December 1985, my boys and I began committing jump-out robberies. (Remember, I said my hoodlum activities ceased *considerably* - not altogether.) We'd cruise in a stolen car and then jump out on unsuspecting people to rob them. With or without guns, we'd strong-arm them.

One cold night on a block in Newark's North Ward, three of us were in a stolen car. Everyone was strapped. We jumped out on a crowd of five individuals who were hanging out near the block's corner, next to a bar. We thought they were selling drugs, which is why we targeted them.

On runs like this, my take-charge disposition came naturally with matters that required action. When committing crimes, I spoke with authority and a non-negotiable tone, and my peers listened to me. Rarely would they question my commands or strategies. I was calm under certain kinds of pressure - the high-intensity, life-on-the-line type of pressure. The OGs (original gangstas or elders who understood crime life) used to tell me, "The military loves guys like you, Dame." That affirmed me a great deal. Since I lived in an urban war zone, I thought I had to behave like a general to ensure the success of our mission.

I told the driver to drop me and the other passenger off at the other end of the block so we could walk up on our five targets. The next instruction was for the driver to pull up on the scene once we had everyone lying down on the ground. The plan went down as I envisioned, with one exception.

A patron came drunkenly stumbling out of the bar that was a house distance away from our robbery scene. The drunk stopped in his tracks, very soberly, and he and I stared at each other for a few seconds before recognition set in. It was Gary, a boyfriend of one of my older female cousins. We spoke no words, but communication was made. Gary calmly did an about-face and went back into the bar. As he did, my accomplice began walking after Gary and telling him, "Don't do it," meaning don't go back inside the bar. I told my boy, "Let him go, we got what we came for." Gary went back inside the bar, and we jumped in our getaway car and sped away.

I wasn't worried about Gary telling the cops it was me. He watched me grow-up and he was one of the Hood OGs/Icons that I hung out with sometimes. I did know Gary would be looking for me either the next day or a couple days later because we hit those dudes for three-hundred bottles of crack and about six-hundred dollars. At my age, this was a major score!

But Cent's messages weighed on me. "This shit I'm doing can't last and can't end well," I thought to myself.

Shortly after that score, I was smoking weed all day and high as a giraffe's ass when I saw the famous commercial for the Marines that extolled: *The Few, The Proud, The Marines*! The slogan impressed me. It moved me. I wanted to be like that disciplined, well-dressed Marine in the commercial who oozed confidence and purpose. I wanted that for myself and knew deep down I needed to get out of Newark to ever get it. Even more providentially, the next day Gary came looking for me. I assumed he wanted a few bottles of free crack from me. We met up in my backyard alone. He was very happy to see me. He was smiling, hugging me and commending me for the take-down the night before.

After a while, I got short-tempered with his brown-nosing. Scornfully I said, “Here! Take these bottles and go!” I slapped them in his hand and tried to send him off. His whole demeanor changed. He seemed hurt and offended. A serious but non-threatening side of him arose. He then said pleadingly, “I came to talk to you.”

“Is that right? About what?,” I asked doubtfully.

“They’re looking for you. The guys you had laid down and robbed the other night …”

Gary cautiously goes on: “Those guys be out there selling for the cops too. Nothing but cops be in that bar I came out of. They wanted to know if I recognized y’all. You know I played dumb. The cops really don’t give-a-fuck because nobody got shot or killed, and the niggas soft as cotton - so you good. But I just wanted to tell you something else because I got a lot of love for you and I watched you grow up. Take your ass to the Army or Marines for a few years and become an MP (military police) then get some training and discipline. Then, come back and be a Newark or East Orange cop. You don't have any convictions; you're Black and from Newark, so they gotta hire you. And then you can lay all these drug selling mother fuckers down on the ground - LEGALLY! That's all I got to say youngblood. Now you can't say nobody never told you. Gary just did."

As he walked down the alleyway from my backyard to the streets, I just looked at him. I was stunned out of my mind in disbelief of what he had just dropped on me. "This gotta be a sign," I told myself. In that moment, I resigned myself to chill out for a year and four months, turn 18 and join the Marines. Now I just have to stay out of trouble. But that would be a hard thing to do when trouble was all around me.

First, I limited my dealings with people. I cut people off. I cut off girlfriends; cut out hanging out time on the avenue. I went to school and even clowned around with old friends, the kind who had career plans. For two months, I was implementing a new strategy and approach for Damon Donnelle Venable.

I was dating a girl named Chrystal who had a baby boy who was seven months old. We spent a lot of time together with her baby in her bedroom. We talked and laughed a lot. Chrystal was the first girl I was really interested in getting serious with, but I cowered and eventually pulled myself away from her emotionally. I honestly didn't think I deserved her. I was crazy about her, though. I would go to school just to see her.

The times I spent with Cent taught me some things about myself and impacted the way I interacted with Chrystal. I had a massive fear of becoming emotionally connected. It terrorized me to know that I really liked a specific girl. That signaled to me when it was time to pull away or dump them altogether.

As a confidant of Cent's, she shared with me that she was sexually abused by both her mother's boyfriend (from ages of eight to 11) and her mother's brother (from ages ten to 14). They would sometimes molest her together. Sickening! One day I remember her telling me some of things they did to her and would make her do - as a child. It disgusted me to my core. I told her I was going to kill her uncle for her. He was a known drunk and hung out in front of a certain corner liquor store in the neighborhood. She pleaded with me not to kill him. Cent begged and cried, so I relented. But I did (I *had* to) beat him down very seriously with a baseball bat and sent him to the hospital for a very long time. (As for her mother's boyfriend, he got killed when Cent was 11. An unsolved murder, she said.)

Cent was so angry with me about her uncle's beat-down. She threatened not to speak or deal with me anymore. She eventually forgave me and we actually became even closer because of it. It prompted me to let down my walls of shame and tell her about my childhood sexual abuse.

Like many young males, I refused to be viewed as a victim of sexual abuse when it's committed by the opposite sex. When I did share what happened to me with other boys or older male cousins while seeking-out their advice, they viewed what happened to me as a badge of honor.

"Why you complaining about that? Shit, nigga, give her my name and address so she can molest me!" In search of help for my confusion, this is what I would hear. Only in a dysfunctional environment and under a jaded identity-concept, could being six years-old and taken advantage of sexually by a woman be touted as something to brag about or confirm a boy's masculinity.

Molestation fucked me up as a child, as a teenager, and well into my late adolescence! I was unaware of the extent of that damage. I later realized it was the core reason I didn't trust people. It adversely affected my family and social relationships. I became detached and withdrawn - and angered by it. Cent helped me recognized that my promiscuity was a manifestation of my confusion, guilt and shame from the sexual abuse I experienced at such a young age. And proneness to violence. What she shared and taught me then couldn't completely heal me or wake me up from my own blinding despair, but the seeds were planted and they helped.

So even with all this understanding I pulled back from Chrystal. She had become a safe haven for me. I was spending so much time with her and Sabur (her son) that it kept me from engaging with reckless people and in dangerous activities. It allowed me to visualize my new plan - to become a Marine at age 18. By this time, I had gotten my beefs under control to the point where I wasn't so tense, or filled with anxiety, or had the need to carry my gun. Some of the individuals I was beefing with got locked up or just disappeared. What I couldn't know then was that this time in my life was the calm before the storm.

1986

In late February of 1986, I decided not to bring my gun to school because I wasn't going to be there all day. I usually go to school just to see Chrystal and make plans for later. I'd sometimes go just to show my face for attendance purposes. I stayed later than I wanted - all the way to 7th period. It's a dangerous period because school is almost over for the day. People start to gather around the school, or near it, in order to meet and pick-up their peeps so they can catch victims coming home from school. I was leaving school with two dudes I infrequently hung-out with. I lived a block-and-a-half from school. It would be a short walk and nothing to worry about today - so I thought. I was four houses away from my house and I spotted the "jump-out boys" heading towards us. They had stick-up intentions telegraphed in every step of their movement. I noticed they were strapped from the way they concealed their hands. I casually turned around to see what was in back of us. It was a car full of hard-faced dudes cruising at walking speed two houses behind us. I urgently told myself, "I gotta make a break for it now!"

I reflectively remember the guys I am with. They are oblivious to the danger that's about to get at us. I talked myself out of running and leaving them, and instead furtively grabbed my money out of my pants pocket and tucked it into my sleeve. I'm visualizing how this robbery is about to go down. They want our coats and jewelry, and will check our pockets for money. They'll time it quickly. The robbery won't take longer than two minutes, maybe less, because school is letting out and people are walking down the street. They approach with guns drawn and announcing, "You know what it is! Give up the coats, money and jewelry and nobody gets shot!" I'm too upset to be scared and fearful for my life.

I think to myself, "These clowns think they had the drop on me. But I seen these mother fuckers coming. And today I left my gun home. Luck is on their side today." I take off my Black leather puffy bomber jacket and one of the robbers takes it. He pats our pockets. They tell us to run. My two associates began running before he completed the command to run. I did an about-face and began coolly walking away. A shot rang out, hitting the pavement next to my foot. I feel the sharp, concrete bits hitting my calves as they ricocheted from the ground where the bullet hit. "I said run nigga," the shooter screamed. I turned toward him, looked him in the eyes and nonchalantly said, "I live right there in that house. I ain't running nowhere. Do what you gotta do!"

The robbers briskly walked toward the car and hopped in. So many people, my neighbors who watched me grow up, came outside to investigate the gun shot; now watched me become a victim of gun violence. Their concern about my safety and health abound. They thought I was shot. My mother, aunts, cousins, everybody came out. I was numb, enraged and overwhelmed. This experience was the final piece to the makings of a me - the juvenile offender.

"Fuck the Marines! Fuck school! Fuck everybody! I ain't safe nowhere! So fuck it!"

From then on, I carried my gun everywhere I went. I would never get caught off-guard again. I did my Hood homework on the robbers. Ed was his name and he was from Bergen Street. I decided I was going to hurt him really bad. I went to his Hood and robbed everybody that I thought resembled him. I was possessed, going up and down his neighborhood looking for him. Two younger guys in my Hood, hearing about my armed pursuits across town, asked to accompany me on one of these hostile excursions. Initially, I said no, but then relented when they offered to provide a stolen car for the trip.

In those days, mobile escapes were convenient when committing the crimes and causing havoc. At the same time, Ed was tipped-off that I was coming for him. So on this brisk, early night in March 1986, I'm cruising in the passenger seat of a stolen car with two individuals I barely know. I'm packing a gun and we've been smoking blunts and drinking beer for about an hour. We were parked on a dark street in Ed's neighborhood, and I abruptly announced, "Aight, take me back across town." The driver starts the car, turns on the lights and pulls off. When the passenger in the backseat says, "Look at those dudes walking down the street. Let's get them before we go home." My mental and emotional state was so upended that my resolve and leadership senses disregarded every sign and inclination to not perform this petty street robbery.

I wavered, consented and said to them, "make it quick." The backseat passenger dolefully replied, "You're not jumping out with me?" In a rush to take my leave of them, the area, and everything else behind me that night, I unthinkingly agreed. I came up with a spontaneous robbery plan for us to execute. "This should be an in-and-out job; they're our age and they shouldn't give us any trouble," I said after giving each their assignment. We accosted the dudes who we targeted and robbed them according to plan. Initially, I felt a sigh of relief going back to the car because there weren't any surprises and it all went down as planned. We're about to get out of here.

As we got closer to the car, a strong voice sounded out, "Hey, give him back his stuff!" A second after that, one of my boys yells, "Oh shit, he's coming towards us!" I pivoted and noticed what appeared to be an angry, somewhat big muscular man approaching me.

In my drug stupor and riddled with youthful impulsivity, I pulled the pilfered items from over the gun I had in my hand - that the man obviously didn't see. Unfortunately, I was locked in military mode from one plan failing and now having to improvise, on the fly. Shooting seemed the only sure-fire response to get away.

Shooting made sense in my irrational mind. Everything that enraged me, angered me, hurt me, disrespected me, abused me, scorned me, bullied me and oppressed me throughout my young life appeared in that instance. After I raised the gun, I shot one time. The horn blows, "Come on man," my cohort yelled at me. I didn't panic but I was frozen emotionally. In a split second so much rage and regret was unleashed from within, time seemed to stand still.

I snapped out of it. The realization of the seriousness of what just took place, what I did to another person, collided with my conscience and consciousness at mind-numbing force. I staggered a bit and jumped in the car. We all parted ways that night not suspecting the gravity of what we did -

what I had done. My action was enormously irreparable. I read in the newspaper two days later, "Man dies from gunshot injuries."

On April 1, 1986, at the age of 16, I was arrested and charged with murder, robbery and gun possession. As hard and unforgiving as my Hood was - as I had become - it paled in comparison to the unforgiving nature and design of the criminal justice system toward Black youths. The system benefited by me killing another Black man. My Black body was now a slave to the criminal legal system of America. Two beautiful Black young men (as described by both mothers) were ripped from the world - from life - for the price of one. I was cased-up and imprisoned, now property of the government. This is so because the 13th Amendment to the United States Constitution abolished slavery and involuntary servitude, *except as punishment for a crime*. The Amendment was authorized by the Senate on April 8, 1864, by the House of Representatives on January 31, 1865, and ratified by the required 27 of the then 36 states on December 6, 1865, and proclaimed on December 18, as history recounts.

The magnitude of the consequences for my murderous actions, alongside the civil and legal conditions I was now under totally escaped my understanding. I suffered a Civil Death, which according to a legal dictionary authority, is the loss of all, or almost all, civil rights by a person due to a conviction for a felony. I was a child now adjudged by the state to be regarded and treated as an adult for prosecution purposes only. To think I was still legally unable to obtain a driver license, buy cigarettes or alcoholic beverages, or open up a savings account without my parents' permission. However, I was officially decreed by the courts to stand trial as an adult. I subsequently went to trial, was found guilty and sentenced to 50-years to Life in prison before my classmates even graduated High School. After my conviction for murder and robbery, still 17 years old, I believed my life was over. I was going to die in prison.

Prison Saved My Life

Ten years into my sentence, little to nothing changed for me. I truly thought my death in prison was inevitable. In the same way I allowed my dysfunctional social environment to shape my mindset and control how I perceived the world and myself, I permitted the prison environment to continue to fashion my mindset in self-defeating ways. This mindset clouded my vision of the future. I couldn't look past the 35 years I had to spend in prison just to be considered for parole. I walked blindly and without purpose; missing all the signs and lessons in my path that could have spared me the pain and scars I experienced.

The next decade of my carceral existence was one saturated in prison violence. I was young and I had put on prison weight. At 19 years-old I weighed 220 lbs on a 5'10" inch frame. I also had the strength that came with my compacted girth. My intellectual capacity matured as well, but my enthusiasm and effort to saturate myself intellectually was elusive. Though I read and was receptive to the instructions from the Prison-Dads (elder men who acted as surrogate fathers for us young prisoners), I was lazy academically. I ran from the challenges of formal education and in doing so I refused to truly empower myself. I was bound to a powerless position and status - a prisoner - and I had let that identity become a self-fulfilled prophecy.

I played the Big Yard (the prison recreation yard) where I worked out, wasted time telling war stories with other young prisoners, smoked weed, and observing/learning the social politics of prison life. Time was doing me when the smarter thing was to do time productively. Thousands of years ago *Pythagoras*, a Greek philosopher, wrote, “Man without education is a savage.” I exemplified this savagery. I had no forward-thinking skills, and so I believed time in the future would be no different than time I was experiencing in the present. This big lie was shown to me by my own ignorance. This lie says, “You are and will always be only what you’ve been through and nothing more.” And so believing in this lie, I descended deeper into my worst self because I felt that I was no longer on a life’s journey in which to learn from the signs and lessons along its path, but that I was firmly at the end-all-be-all final destination in my life. A living hell!

It was perhaps at this point that I had learned that hope is the inner force and power that allows a person to restrain their worst self and keep that part of them subdued. Simply put, I had to find a way to let in some hope. This was easier said than done because of my imprisoned, indifferent mindset. I was without hope and education, and because of my savagery I eventually became a feared prison gangsta. I robbed, fought and extorted other prisoners as with a commitment to be fulfilled and affirmed daily. It wasn't ignorance that motivated my savagery because I knew better. I was raised by decent, lovely Black folk.

Inside I chose not to care or be brave enough to act in the manner in which I was raised. My failure to care led me to even fight with prison guards and threaten prison staff. I had a death wish that was operating below my conscious awareness. Deep down, I believed I was walking and living in my coffin every day. I had a viewpoint that there was no need to embrace a love for life and the lessons acquired from overcoming adversity. I've since learned that the opposite of love isn't hate - it's more close to indifference. There were no guns in prison, except those carried by the tower guards. So I had no fear of confrontation in prison because I didn't have to worry about getting shot unless I tried to escape. Fighting was my best problem resolution skill because I was angry, confused and scared to both be my true self, and also envision a promising future for myself. Being guided by my indifference and ignorance required me, as most professionals have acknowledged, to become a poor decision maker, full of resentment and bitterness, engage in interpersonal conflicts, waste time and resources, walk without purpose, miss the signs and opportunities for real personal and lifelong progress. I was a waking theory of dysfunctionality.

A life-changing quote for me reads, "Adversity introduces a man to himself." So at 18, I was thrown into gladiator school. In 1987, I entered Trenton State Prison to do my life sentence. At that time the prison still had a national reputation for the level of violence that took place within it by both the guards and the prisoners. Violence was so naturalized in that space that it became the subject of scholarly study. Gresham M. Sykes, an American criminologist, studied Trenton State Prison (now New Jersey State Prison). His work has been described as a "pioneering look at the issues faced by guards as well as the pains of imprisonment encountered by inmates," by academic professionals.

Unfortunately I lived, experienced and, thankfully, survived the very conditions and environment that Sykes studied and observed to develop the *Pains of Imprisonmen*t theory. From the ages of 18 until 28, I was introduced to an inner-self that perfected prison violence by way of repetitious practice. I had met a version of myself at this time that was young in every aspect of being young. I realized that I had the mindset of a zombie—I was a dead man walking who didn't give a fuck!

It's a frightening experience to see yourself at your lowest inner state of being while you are also in the nethermost place or condition that life has to offer. These conditions don't demand the experience of prison life in order for one to descend towards their vilest self; it only requires having a mindset that imprisons one to hopelessness. In situations like this, people find all kinds of justifications to become their most horrible selves. I encountered these persons first-hand because the prison universe manufactures hopelessness. Despair is endemic to prison as trees are to a forest. I became aware of this when I realized that most of my violent encounters were with individuals who were totally dark inside and lived as if wanting a suicide-by-inmate experience. Losing my own battles with despair I had *nearly* obliged their death wishes. These were incarcerated men who blocked all rays of hope from shining within and were violently (or suicidally) groping their way through life.

When hope is lost and despair becomes the sole proprietor of one's soul, one personifies a figurative living death. I was dead inside and seemingly inert. Despite this morbid mindset that dictated my life, my parents never ceased supporting me nor stopped being nurturing and loving to me. One particular proof of the love from my parents had become the pivotal, resurrecting moment in my life.

My mom and dad remained committed to bringing the family on contact visits, writing letters to me and ensuring that my younger sisters wrote letters to me also. They kept the phone available to accept collect calls, despite the exorbitant, predatory pricing rates. My family had become my proverbial lifeline to humanity. Their demonstrated love ultimately implanted a ray of hope inside me. As my mother would often say, "We don't have much in life but we got a lot of love."

The struggles and sacrifices my parents willfully endured to ensure that I felt their love was my wake-up call to change myself. Despite a life sentence in prison with little possibility of ever returning to society, they loved me through it. There was one defining moment that transformed my selfish mentality. I'm proud that I finally got a clue and my self-absorbed and self-limiting mindset shifted to a selfless, loving and compassionate person. I was doubly confined; I was in physical prison and a personal prison. But my transformation occurred as a result of my mom's reaction to what she thought was a loss of my contact visits for life.

In the prison universe, the authorities keep control over their captives with a collection of proverbial carrot-on-a-stick rules and privileges.

My selfishness was completely called into question the day I received an institutional sanction for getting caught with some weed. The sanction was a *permanent* loss of contact visitation privileges that can be restored after a year and the completion of a substance abuse program *if* it was the first sanction for a drug charge. This was my first and only drug charge inside prison. My mom was unaware of this because I got into so much trouble. I sent the sanction sheet home to her with the intention of explaining everything before the mail arrived. The mail got to her before I could call. That phone call with her is indelibly stained in my memory and became the launching point of my journey toward inner hope. She accepted the call, and the first words from her were, "Oh, my God! I'm never going to touch you again!" She believed that - deeply.

The system describes things like visitation as a privilege because prisoners have very few rights. Guards have to respect these privileges but they can be forfeited by an arbitrary decision by prison personnel for the slightest offense. In practice it's the modern-day equivalent of *Plessy v. Ferguson,* The U.S. Supreme Court decision that ruled a Black man had no rights in which a white person needed to respect and also legitimize the practice of racial segregation in the United States under the absurd standard of "separate but equal." Laws that are written by systems of oppression to keep others subjugated over time simply get recycled and reused. The prison administration had implemented Draconian rules (many of which were/are rooted to the very same absurdly racist legal rationale used to enslave and subjugate Blacks) during the excessively punitive prison era of mass incarceration. The powers that be wanted to hurt the families of incarcerated-individuals who violated their rules. Even smoking a joint would incur the permanent loss of visit privileges of a prisoner, as was the case with me.

Finally, by age 28, I had overcome my own negative perspective on education and an inability to see past the present moment, beyond my personal prison. I started this breakthrough when I earned my GED (General Education Diploma) some years earlier. Later, I focused on getting certificates in barbering, paralegal studies, typing, poetry, mathematics, second language, and computer literacy, just to name a few. I also began loving the idea of challenging my intellectual capabilities and excelling in the classroom. I found out I was extraordinarily good at mathematics (calculus, trigonometry, geometry, pre-calculus, etc.) and had a knack to understand dense, abstract philosophical writings and theories. I realized that in order to free myself from my imprisoning mindset, I had to truly educate myself.

In life we are inevitably presented with situations that entail us to make some critical choices that affect and determine our present and future condition. Prison life is no exception. While in prison, where time is bountifully conducive to both personal reformation and also deformation, I chose education as my pathway to reform myself. These accomplishments were always just pleasantly accepted by my mom, and no big emotional displays of a proud and surprised mama came from her. Her response to my sending or telling her of my educational or vocational achievements were reserved and delivered in a monotone, "Yeah, I always knew that about you." Oddly, her reactions would become the bread crumbs guiding me towards a part of myself I neglected—my emotional self.

Love Sparks Hope

I have often heard the saying, "*Love is the most powerful force in the world,*" but I never really believed it. That all changed after hearing the fear, heartbreak and disappointment in my mother's voice as she agonized about never being able to touch her Baby Boy again. In that moment I not only became a believer in the *Power of Love,* I also became a beneficiary of it. My mother's love was the irresistible force that moved me to transcend my selfishness, indifference, weakness and inability to see beyond my present constraints and painful moments. It was at this point in my life I began to see and believe that I could (or had to) rise above my circumstances. My life literally and figuratively commenced the dawning of an existential conversion. I woke up from a living dream of despair. Now only physically imprisoned, I was freed from my personal prison. It felt like my coffin door had opened up and the light from it now enabled my imaginations to exist farther in time and greater in wonderful possibilities.

I began altering everything I did, said, thought, felt and believed in a more self-critical and self-correcting way. What I experienced was more than a transformation or change. In the words of Victor Hugo, in *Les Miserables*, in describing the complete change of Jean Valjean, the protagonist, "It was a transfiguration!" I had totally metamorphosed my mindset to something completely different in form, structure and function akin to a butterfly, after being cocooned, is different in every aspect from the caterpillar it once was.

I realized that such a transfiguration was possible from the many anecdotal, philosophical, historical, and literary examples of human transformation. One poignant and dear example for me then was the Christian Apostle Paul who once was Saul, the ruthless bounty hunter and persecutor of Christians for the Romans. I finally realized from these examples (which were always there in my life, and I view in hindsight as the signs I missed) that I grew up feeling helpless. I believed I was worthless because I wasn't courageous enough to neither take ownership of my actions nor embrace accountability and responsibility. For so long I had subscribed to a false identity that precluded me from admitting I was wrong - period point blank.

There is an integral connection between identity and accountability. Identity is who you say you are, and accountability is what people know you to be through your actions. My perception began to drastically change because my attitudes, beliefs and knowledge grew and matured. I felt a sense of positive self-authority overtaking me from this change. I was committed to relentlessly pursuing more of it. I knew that I had to start being honest with myself. I had to develop an ability to stay inexorably focused and disciplined in this pursuit of empowering myself.

Imagine being imprisoned for ten years and still having - at minimum - 25 years more to go. That was me. 25 years before I could even be considered for parole (which has a 92% denial rate for first time eligibility). But I now believed in my capacity for redemption and wholeheartedly believed in my redeeming spirit. I had hope, for a change. I would now live in a way that dismantles America's myth about Black men and Black Boys irredeemable nature. There was an 8% chance of me getting paroled in 25 years, so that meant freedom was possible. But that's the funny thing or nature about hope, it's almost never present in a little bit.

Let's say, for argument's sake, that hope can be present in little measure. I'd then argue that because hope's metaphysical power is so concentrated and capable of producing strong effects, similar to the physical power of concentrated pieces of Uranium that fuels nuclear power plants, ships and bombs, that hope can never truly exist as something measly.

Hope compelled me to believe I was worthy and deserving of a second chance. Hope fueled my inward journey toward a better self, toward developing a relationship and understanding with my Higher Power, toward discovering my purpose and potential, and toward accepting my spiritual gifts. Gifts I knew I had to use and not just to benefit myself.

Although my perceptions were transformed, broadened and expanded, the reality of my confinement was fixed, unchanged and outwardly permanent. It was harsh and cruel, and unforgiving as the name implies - the pains of imprisonment. My confinement and being written-off by society tore daily through every shred of my soul. I had become resolved to make my captivity a cocoon and emerged redeemed, and anew. I would clutch the cloistered qualities of prison life and extract all its monastic elements because my life depended on it. I realized that although I was young and still in the adolescent developmental stage of my life - which explains my impulsivity, impetuousness, inability to utilize my higher executive functions and most of all succumbing to internal emotional hijackings that makes young persons very irrational at times - I simply became averse to challenges and truly lacked discipline.

It's commonly understood in academic thought that "perception may be controlled by external factors, but reality cannot be controlled by anyone or anything. However, it should be noted that not all perceptions are wrong. Sometimes, our perception may reflect reality itself," see (www.differencebetween.com). So through the immeasurable power of hope I began conceptualizing the walls that encased me and the bars that constrained me, the institution of prison (my uncontrollable reality), as my monastery - my figurative cocoon.

I reasoned that I was so distant from the best version of myself, and there were ample recorded proofs to confirm it and would be used against me in trying to attain freedom, that I had to virtually, if not realistically, walk the path akin to a monk for the next 25 years. I began to steel myself mentally against both my inner negative thoughts and the negative external forces. Both of these forces together I viewed as my crucible, my trial by fire. I had taken a vow to myself to abstain from violent actions, drug use, or any behaviors that were non-conducive to securing my freedom. Through this, I'd have to learn the true value of sacrifice, effort, humility, patience, discipline and determination in action. Hope would lead the way. These action-oriented values would be difficult to implement under optimal circumstances. I was pessimistic about being able to abide as a monk in hostile territory such as prison life. But it was my only option and my best preparatory tool for sculpting and shaping my character and mindset into something (someone) redeemable, and ready to live amongst the free in society.

The journey of a thousand footsteps began with the first step. My destination was more than two decades away and its actuality was unknown and uncertain. I didn't even focus on its possibility of being obtained. I just believed that it had to happen. Hope said it had to. Where I once was an insecure, self-doubting, impressionable, indecisive kid who waywardly went in the direction of the winds of social pressures and influences, I now had to become a man intentionally directing his decisions by a sure sense of self-confidence, purpose, discipline, faith, and a belief in his own redemption.

A Buddist creed states: *To master the universe outside, one must first master the universe inside.* This was motivation and a source of inspiration to daily and meditatively reflect inwardly. I became an excavator of my own soul, mind, and heart with intentions on breaking past the gut-wrenching fear most people have of acknowledging their faults, weaknesses, or shameful base desires. I fearlessly embarked towards the deep recesses of my psyche on a mission of self-correction, self-healing. I had to learn how to coach, mentor and encourage myself through this uncomfortable process of seeking out the worst parts of myself that made me who I am in order to transform.

It would take nothing short of purposefully self-directed, inward action to accomplish this. However, prison is an immersive space of hostility and inhumanity that possesses very limited motivational resources. There are too many forces pulling the human spirit where it shouldn't enter. Prison is both a hyper-reality space of violence, misery, anguish and disillusionment, and also a place of temporal flux that makes your past always your present and future experience. Books became one of my primary and greatest motivational sources, and guided my spirit above the ruckus of the prison universe. They revealed to me that I made poor decisions in life, ran from adversity, and became distracted by my physical appetites because I was without self-discipline. That I wasn't using my capacity for reasoning to reign over my lower, selfish desires. I failed to realize that what other people thought about me had little to no importance.

A sign of intelligence is being able to use indirect knowledge and experience in a wise and self-beneficial manner. I study the philosophers, historians, theologians, educators, researchers, scholars and others to collect indirect knowledge and experience. Particularly, I enjoy the authors of the Black Renaissance as they were intellectual thinkers and powerful writers. Their work spoke to me! The way they wielded words resonated loudly, strongly and profoundly within me. It was as if their experiences were mine; a feeling of Déjà vu. I was both the character Bigger Thomas, Damon Cross, and Richard Wright's *Black Boy*. I was positively overwhelmed by the "constant rage" expressed in *The Fire Next Time* by James Baldwin. My humanity had been invisible just as Ralph Ellison wrote.

Although my body had been shackled and limited spatially, I knew my mind couldn't be limited.

To be limited in its growth and accumulation of knowledge meant the end of me. I reasoned that in order to transform I must develop characteristics and qualities that facilitate personal transformation. One quality I adopted was a pleasure from reading. This simple act served many purposes but two important ones were: 1) it advanced my knowledge. I turned that know-how into lessons and wisdom I could live off of and share; and 2) it curtailed my wants for bodily/sexual pleasure and it made it easy for me to control those urges in the non-heterosexual space of prison.

Reading became my sustenance and gave me self-control. I continued to grow to understand myself. Critical self-reflection brought me to the realization that I was in prison because I wasn't acquainted deeply enough with my abilities or talents. As a result I made some truly bad choices. I wasn't fully aware of my weaknesses or familiar enough with my fears though I was ruled by them. Most Black young men are taught to neglect our emotional side and not see it as a strong and an important aspect of ourselves. I didn't know myself but I now had 25 years to identify and allay my weaknesses and fears. This needed to be done strategically and methodically. Collecting wisdom from other people's scars became a commitment and a challenge for me.

I once read about a brutal conquistador during the age of Europe's exploration (or subjugation and colonization) of North America - the so-called New World. After this conquistador and his legion of ships landed on the shore, he ordered all the ships to be burned. He did this to inspire a sense of urgency, cohesion and commitment within his army. He also wanted to instill an all-or-nothing, no-retreat attitude about the dangers they would face. I had to use the no-retreat lesson of this historical account in my own journey of self-exploration. I couldn't turn back; I wouldn't run away from the shameful things I'd uncover about myself.

Fortunately, I knew enough about myself and was honest enough with myself to know I had a great deal of emotional baggage to unpack. It required encountering some hard, ugly truths with the same toughness and gangsta attitude I applied outwardly toward my enemies and my hyper-masculine identity. I would now use it to deal with the ugly parts. I critiqued my actions so I could organize my beliefs, mindset, and purpose to ***not*** continue down a path of insanity. I wanted to avoid what Socrates said, "The undisciplined life is an insane life."

Regaining sanity over savagery was the goal; my life and freedom depended on it. Renovating myself was critical on so many levels. I had to smartly prepare for all of the contingencies associated with surviving prison. At the same time, having the will to better myself, seek redemption and earn the right to be a free human being meant I could become someone who had something to positively contribute to society.

Imagine embarking on a journey that would last for the next twenty five years, minimum. "That's a long goddam time to prepare for something not guaranteed," I often thought to myself. "How will I succeed? How will I make it through this journey made of decades of time mixed with the unknown?" My confidence in achieving victory through this complex prospect waivered, but I now had hope and faith in my abilities.

Let's be clear. My hope and faith were surely the size of mustard seeds. Together, though, they empowered me to imagine success for myself - not just in the future but also for the present. Despite the fact I was a lifer in a prison cell with no education, no money, no social status, and no rights that law enforcement had to respect. I looked at the world differently and became willing to recondition my outlook. I decided that success was my future and that good character would now become my social currency and gateway to existential wealth.

A Paradigm Shift

Life is a process of continual relearning and one's environment is essential to our cognitive outcomes, or what we learn over and over; and, more importantly, how we proceed from it. My talents, skill sets, potential and gifts were all robbed from the world, my family, my community, and me because I left my environment due to a lack of belief in and knowledge of myself. I undertook a complete revision of myself during this cocooned period. I had to make prison into an environment that cultivated self-empowerment. I would change everything about me that wasn't conducive to my becoming a success as an individual, whether my fate was that I died in prison or obtained freedom.

The key to my transfiguration would be the reconstruction of my mind. Successful people have a mindset committed to doing what others are unwilling to do. I've learned that successful people expect to be successful and believe in their abilities and talents so strongly that they are willing to act on that belief via their daily performances. This process of reconditioning my mind towards a successful one required me to be mindful every waking and sleeping hour of every good and bad experience, or encounter, and how I wanted to view myself.

Prison is a structure that encapsulates hopelessness and despair, so one of my greatest challenges was to daily affirm and believe in my own self-worth despite my immersion in a space of physical misery and emotional trauma. I mastered sublimation. A skill I characterize as *Existential Jujitsu* because it required me to learn that provocation isn't always offensive, tension isn't always negative or painful, and conflict isn't always dangerous to us. We've heard the saying, "Life is about struggle!" I'm a firm believer that anything worth having in life shouldn't come easy. Adversity is a way in which one meets their higher self. Struggle is what refines us; it distills our character into something substantive and invaluable.

Fundamentally, this constitutes the struggle of life. If you want something bad enough, put in the work, effort and sacrifice to achieve it. In expecting and wanting a successful life for myself, I began a practice of living life through the acceptance that provocation is sometimes needed for us to act in opposition to our fears and what's comfortable. Tension is just creative energy that we haven't given an outlet; and, conflict is simply meaning that hasn't been made understood. The benefit and purpose of this practice is to take over my own narrative.

For systems of oppression to successfully implement the project of Mass Incarceration, it had to disseminate a false narrative of Black and poor young people for society to accept. Society could then feel good about itself in having written-off people, like me, as irredeemable and not fit to live as a human being in society. It's very dehumanizing to have others write your narrative. They essentially define you to the world. The process was crafted during times of slavery and Jim Crow segregation. Today it just has a different name.

I grew to understand that one of the sources of angst and disapproval by revolutionary Black and non-Black folks is the practice of social promotion. Shamefully, I appreciated it during my high school years because it allowed me to focus on earning a rep at the cost of learning aesthetic judgment and how to textually and articulately construct my best self. A common understanding of social promotion is the practice of school systems promoting a student to the next grade after a school year, regardless if they learned the necessary material or if they are often absent, see (https://en.m.wikipedia.org/wiki/Social_promotion). This practice was more often put into action than grade retention, which held students back a grade for not attending school or not learning the material. Some education circles believe the retention practice to be counterproductive. In urban schools that already had a great high school drop-out rate among poor Black students, it was not a cost-effective response to poor performance. There were cheaper interventions, such as summer schools or tutoring programs (Ibid, Social Promotion cite.)

Whether in 1985, 2005 or 2025, such a practice is non-conducive to character building, albeit more humane than the "School to Prison Pipeline" that would come later. One historical research authority says, "The school-to-prison pipeline is when schools criminalize minor infractions that result in student exposure to the criminal justice system. A disproportionate number of these children are people of color, and once they are in the school-to-prison pipeline, it becomes increasingly difficult to provide them with the education they so desperately need to be successful. This often leads to recidivism and a life filled with instability and poverty," see (The School-to-Prison Pipeline: Definition, Examples & Implications | Study.com). I mention these truths because they explain a lot of the past and present social dysfunctions taking place in poor Black cities.

As a direct recipient of the practice, I recognized I didn't have to apply myself academically and I'd still pass-on to the next grade. It caused me to falsely believe in myself that I had not only learned the material to proceed on, but that I earned the grade advancement. Social promotion also instilled a practice of not challenging my intellect. Reflecting back on my experiences, this practice zapped my inquisitiveness to learn useful educational lessons or reading literature that forges noble characteristics and dreams within young minds. Taking the easy route in life was expected of me and encouraged by the very professionals tasked with my learning and development into a productive social being. That mindset and my complacent ways contributed to landing me behind bars, and unable to write my own narrative.

Black young men have been depicted as criminal in every way. I became determined to set myself on a path to re-appropriate authorship of my own narrative and take control over my life. I would do this by pursuing commitments that transcend my own life so as to be of and in service to others. I could no longer be a slave to my own inner prisons. To continue living this way would be to confirm the narratives about me that are written by others. I had to develop a just attitude, get past my own suffering, become in tune with my spirit, take ownership and responsibility for my behavior and look for signs that success leaves for us to follow in order to stop operating or living below my ability.

I love the saying, "Hard times call for soft skills." Soft skills are universally defined to be personal attributes that enable a person to interact effectively and harmoniously with others. I was locked in a place that could arguably be considered as "hard times." Paradoxically, the success of my journey to freedom would undoubtedly depend on my people and social skills, i.e. soft skills. This is what my monastical approach and training made me master as preparation for the challenges of both attaining freedom and thriving from it.

On May 4, 2021, I was granted parole on my first eligibility. The commitments I made to myself pushed me to open-up to truth; to be true to myself. I courageously became my authentic self and, most importantly, I became a humble man empowered with the faith and willingness to overcome a 92% parole denial rate. I don't attribute luck to this accomplishment. It was my unwavering expectation of getting paroled and the commitment to doing exactly what I needed to do to achieve it. I wanted it, dreamed about it, prepared for it, and affirmed it into existence daily with words and thoughts. They say life is about what you make it - Mine is living proof of it!

New Beginning

I exited prison on May 4, 2021, and was met by cheering supportive family members, friends, strangers, and lawyers. I was mentally stunned by the extreme contrast between the momentousness of sudden freedom and vastness of the open space I just stepped into and the painfully constraining and tortuous space I just stepped out from. I didn't cry though my body and mind wanted to. My stoic discipline froze me emotionally and I just observed all the happy faces, and said "thank you" in response to all the welcoming expressions from my supporters. I felt sensations I never experienced, or perhaps just don't remember ever before experiencing them. I felt as if I was instantly transported into another realm. I was an alien because everything about freedom seemed unknown to me, except the air.

I remember being happy about breathing. It was the weirdest and best experience of my life. While in prison I discovered how to use humor and various art forms to help me make sense of life. I found that it is completely fine and healthy to engage in self-talk because shouldn't one's visions of the future be accompanied and complemented by audio? Reading taught me how to use self-dialogue as a way to protect and strengthen my mental health. In trying to make sense of the abrupt clash of realities and its effects on me upon exiting prison, I thought to myself, "This is what it must have felt like for Neo when he first stepped out of the Matrix."

I had learned over the decades to maintain my poise and not react thoughtlessly or emotionally to high intensity occasions. But on this day I remember being frightened by the thought that the easy part, achieving freedom, was now over and how this was the first day of the beginning of the hardest part of success - maintaining it! My first day of freedom was a mind-numbing experience from the interplay of awkwardness and joyfulness. The awkward feeling was that nothing about freedom felt familiar to me; it was too strange. The difficulty in trying to reconcile this paradox wreaked havoc on my mind. My existentialist leanings taught me that a human being is an embodied freedom. That is, we are constructed with a purpose and intentionality to make our choices and produce our own meaning and values.

The magnitude of my trauma from long-term imprisonment slapped the "fuck out of me," dazed me, and even intimidated me. When I realized the inhumanity of being severed from freedom, it became an existential conflict of epic proportion. I quickly maintained my composure because I trusted myself to reconcile it and find meaning from it but even still I felt like a baby in a man's body. I was inverted and cast into a perceptual void that was seemingly unhinging my mind from my body. However, the joyful feeling came from the momentous occasion and all the wonderful possibilities that it offers. This day was a long time coming and I couldn't enjoy it to its maximum potential. The scars from long-term prison life were glaringly evident to me. I was emotionally repressed and too self-conscious of being overly expressive.

It dawned on me quickly that I walked out of one struggle I had conquered into a new, unfamiliar set of struggles that quickly needed to be identified. It's said that you solve most of a problem the moment you identify it. Initially, it was a daunting task and somewhat robbed me of the happy experience of newly found freedom. But my forward-thinking, vision and commitment to success was on overdrive and I was contemplating and strategizing on what I needed, how to get it and how to use what I got for present and future benefits. I didn't have time for a pity party for myself. I left prison with $5,500 dollars, a birth certificate and a room at my sister's house. I had a supportive family, three college degrees and a few vocational skill certificates. Most notably I had a determined attitude to succeed.

My educational ammunition and resources weren't enough to ease my concerns about my future. I set the bar extremely high as it related to goals. They were clearly lofty, downright noble even. I fixed them high because even if I could partially obtain them I'd still be in a good position. I believed that mediocrity was beneath me. I survived 35 years in a dehumanizing pressure cooker and if pressure creates diamonds, I knew that I could produce a man whose determination, character, and resolve shined hard like one. Some hard truths began sinking in and made me realize how much I didn't know about life and the world. I didn't consider this a second chance at life. Realistically, this was my first opportunity because I was a child the first time around. I never was an adult in a free society and now I must learn how to be one - fast!

As the days of my new found freedom ticked forward so did my confidence in transitioning successfully. I had read many books and spoke with many people about the challenges of reentering society. During my time inside, I asked questions about how to best prepare for release. A glaring truth is that there is no blueprint for successful reentry. As subjective and unique as our individual lives are, so too are individual responses and plans. Mike Tyson said in response to a question about his plans for a fight, "Everybody has a plan until they get hit." This resonated so deeply with me that it changed the course of my reentry preparation. I reasoned that because there are too many things or variables I don't know about society, any plan I create must have contingency plans. Then it got very complicated coming up with a Plan B if Plan A failed, and Plan C if Plan B failed. I set a plan to create a very long list of accomplishments to achieve once I was released. These accomplishments would be my measuring tape for success.

There's a concept called *Societal Rush.* which is the sudden social, financial, familial, and legal pressures that an individual just returning or reentering society will immediately encounter. I viewed the *Societal Rush* phenomenon as the counter hit or force to one's plans that Mike Tyson referred to. I felt confident about my overall mental preparation before release, but I wasn't confident about the State's adherence to their obligations of assisting me in my reentry.

Personal stories were many from individuals who had recidivated, in part, from the awful neglect and abandonment of critical reentry support services by the very state agencies that are funded to provide reentry services and support for Returning Citizens. Before individuals leave prison, the NJDOC social services department is mandated to begin reentry preparation for prisoners 6 months before their exit date. The most crucial aspect of this preparation is to ensure prisoners exit with a non-driver state identification (ID) or with the legal documents needed to help them get a valid state ID once released. Even after lessons from decades of bad reentry experiences and mismanagement - and despite tens of millions of dollars allocated to state and private reentry services agencies - I left the State prison system without any valid state ID or the complete set of legal documents to prove who I was so that I could obtain an ID.

I felt I was set up to fail by the system. The system was angry I survived every blow it threw trying to destroy my humanity. Perhaps it was angry at me because my exiting prison meant that my body was no longer generating approximately $60,000 a year to its multi-billion dollar annual budget. Caring about other people's feelings stopped being a concern of mine a very long time ago. My focus lay in my beliefs about myself and what I wanted for me. The system preys on the foolishness of a person. Relishes it. Depends on it. I'd be a foolish man to have believed that the very system that labeled and treated me as irredeemable would have a desire to diligently help me with all their resources and reentry preparation initiatives on my behalf.

Fortunately, my own preparation proved to be an invaluable asset in my transition. My post-release mindset aided me greatly during the initial phase of my transition. It's possible my transition phase may take as long as the time I spent in prison. I'm not concerned about it, though. I'm highly motivated to succeed and overcome all the barriers that could come against my success - internal and external. At the heart of my mindset lies the inspiration that I overcame, and will overcome, any obstacle before me.

I have a sure belief in my ability to persevere through both known and unknown challenges. Life for me is like climbing a mountain - I know there's a top to it that has everything I desire to flourish. Though I can't see the top of the mountain as I struggle to get there, I'm motivated to climb. I have chosen to allow struggle to strengthen me while I endure the pain. The fact that I can visualize my success has me believing in it without question. I've learned that success is an outcome of the choices we make. With confidence, I'm headed toward the crest of my success. If you are choosing to recondition your mindset toward your own success, then look up, look over and you'll see me there. The laws of attraction are socially most evident in that realm. Successful people enjoy doing life together.

Invaluable Life Lessons

This book's purpose is to give voice to the hundreds of thousands of young, poor Black and marginalized bodies treated cruelly within this country's unjust legal system. The struggles they face, like I faced, are excruciating as they attempt to keep their humanity intact. Sharing the life lessons I learned through these agonizing struggles can help others overcome the internal and external challenges (personal and mental prisons) to personal success, no matter within an actual prison or self-imposed one.

Although the "corrections" system continues to fail our children, I've also learned there's nothing more important than overcoming our own "failures." Motivational speakers and preachers all extol the virtue of not fearing to fail. This is important because failure is but a step towards success. We must learn to fail successfully and gracefully. That simply means to fail upward in life and not downward. Do not be deterred from the possibility of failing to reach for your dreams and ambitions. Recognize that the hardest fight or most challenging endeavor proves to be the most rewarding because what is gained comes from perseverance, persistence and dogged determination.

An exemplary example of these as priceless qualities of successful people is displayed in the story of Thomas Edison, the inventor. He endured thousands of experimental failures before successfully inventing the light bulb. Each failure made him determined to try again and again. He sieved lessons from each failure, too, pushing him to make the next attempt with more confidence and wisdom. This quality demonstrates how time can be maximized to create excellent opportunities to achieve.

Successful people are known for being persistent creatures of habit and ingenuity. They are motivated to learn new things and ardently persevere through difficult times. For some, perseverance is a natural reaction to adversity. And time is viewed as a great commodity - especially when wisely invested into themselves. Determined people neither waste time nor make excuses. Wasting time in their eyes is worse than wasting money. Their mindset doesn't allow them to. The excuses that some make are just sentiments meant to mask their inability to do, achieve or change something. They are sentiments that represent a mindset clouded by fear and led astray by a lack of self-confidence. It is a mindset that becomes content with what one has and where one is in life. The successfully driven person lives in a mindset where limitations and barriers cannot be accepted.

Maya Angelou said (paraphrased), "If you want something to change, change it. If you can't change it, change your attitude." Whatever your prison in life (carceral, emotional, mental, etc.) you have the ability to both break free from it and also thrive from it by changing your perception and attitude towards it, and yourself. I am a living testimonial of Maya Angelou's words. My imprisonment placed physical constraints and limitations on me. Every day I wanted to change my reality. When I had an attitude of accepting my limitations as my lot in life, I was essentially a slave to my excuses and a believer in my inability to be better than I was. Nothing changed because my attitude did not change. Being trapped in any kind of prison is to be trapped in a daily, incessant state of pain, humiliation, fear and anger. These negative states empower a self-defeating attitude. It makes life feel like something to be tolerated instead of being enjoyed or lived.

When I stopped viewing life as something to be tolerated but to be lived and self-actualized, I began seeing my limitations as quests to be pursued in order to gain the knowledge, wisdom, talent and faith I need to be a living success story. Changing my attitude and my perception while in the grasp of state sponsored despair and cruelty is perhaps the best and most courageous decision I made in my life. It is because it showed me the wisdom in accepting life on life's terms, by not living in a state of constant resistance both to others and my own self.

If you feel disempowered by the constraints that surround you, remember this life-impacting fact: Your success is so dependent on your mindset because constraints - if viewed confidently as challenges to be conquered - can be the originator of your unlimited creative energy. The very things that hinder you can also become the source of your escape. The power of your mindset may not concretely change the conditions you are in overnight or over even a period of time. Undoubtedly, though, your thinking will empower you through viewing and approaching those conditions in a manner that constantly provokes and engages your creative imaginations. For instance, in spite of my being immersed for three and a half decades in prison conditions marked by "high rates of suicide, suicide attempts, deadly prisoner-on-prisoner violence, less than adequate medical services, glaring abuses by prison personnel and deadly guard-on-prisoner violence resulting in countless deaths of prisoners year in and year out" I never stopped believing that I would be a success story the world must know about (Stevens, Bryan. *Just Mercy*. One World Publishing; New York. 2014). I had a purpose to survive!

My conditions tried to infect me daily with a dream-killing disease, a self-defeating attitude, and a reason to give up hope, but my mindset gave me an emotional, mental and spiritual immunity to it. To immunize yourself from the negative energies of your adverse conditions and state of mind, commit and daily affirm to yourself - I am better than this! I may not know what your "this" is but I made sure to define my "this". When I did, I wrote it on my vision board and stuck it on my cell wall. Even while in the midst of witnessing deaths as if it were just another normal day while hearing men on the brink of hopelessness and desperation, I had my vision board to look at. That board was my cheerleader. With the grace and blessings of the Higher Power and Great Ancestors, I now have the board on my bedroom wall as a partially free man. Always there as a reminder to be ever cognizant of my vision for success with a monk-like discipline in pursuit of it.

I believe a lack of discipline is the major reason why so many people live unfulfilling lives. In a world that conditions us to become consumers, instant gratification is the normal course of behavior and natural attitude among people. Discipline is not easily acquired because it goes against people's natural inclinations. Reconditioning your mindset from being enslaved by instant gratification is critical. Existentially speaking, life is about reconciling the contradictions we experience as human beings - physical/metaphysical, emotional/rational, pleasure/pain, joy/suffering. With respect to discipline, which is fundamentally necessary to success, Mike Tyson said, "Discipline is doing something you hate, as if you love it!" To display that level of disciplined commitment requires a tandem of motivational factors. These are external and internal sources of motivation.

Many people don't have an internal source of motivation that is powerful enough to move them in ways that are crucially important to experience a fulfilling, successful life. Having external sources (i.e. faith, family, friends, affirmations) are good and essential to pursuing one's goals. However, they are woefully inadequate by themselves. They are more effective in concert with internal sources of motivation. Do you have an inner voice that inspires you, positively egging you on toward your best self? That voice peps you up when difficulties are robbing you of confidence to pursue your personal goals, desired achievements and ambitions. When I was a hoodlum, that voice that pepped me up was for no-good. My new inner voice encourages me toward greatness with goodness.

I once heard from a very successful and remarkably talented woman who was speaking about ways in which people become successful. She said, "You have to be your best cheerleader!" This struck a chord with me because she verbalized exactly what I came to realize years earlier through authors and my own honest self-appraisals. I believe one of the reasons why so many people murder their inner cheerleader is because they have no belief in their abilities. This manifests as a lack of confidence and complete unfamiliarity with the amazing aspects of themselves.

Within you is amazingness! Yours is a reflection of your accomplishments, and without them you have no confirmation of your success or potential of success. If you are not aware of your amazingness, which can be seen as reflections of your accomplishments, then you have nothing proof-positive to function as confirmation of your success or your potential for success. Having a healthy sense of self-esteem, pride and self-image can either grow this proof or wither from its absence. There's a clear and present danger to your mindset when you lack these internal motivations. It can become a vicious, perpetuating negative cycle because without them success is rarely achieved. And because "people who are not successful in the terms understood by their own societies are not respected" by its social systems, leading to further rooting of negative and self-defeating feelings, success is almost guaranteed to elude them (Cleary, Thomas. *Strategies of Counsel.* Vol. 3. Shambala: Boston, Ma. (2000).

What are you doing to be successful, to achieve your goals and to accomplish your ambitions for success? I began asking myself these questions when I stopped being that person who was always saying, "*I'm going* to get into shape when the summer time comes; or, *I'm going* to stop smoking next year." *I'm going* to do almost never gets done! Our desire is strong to do these things but our mindset isn't in a resourceful state. The mindset to achieve is what helps us get the motivation to act on a particular want.

Over time we can give up pursuing an important dream or goal of ours. That surrender becomes our go-to reaction and, unfortunately, replaces the action of doing. We strip ourselves of the benefits and glory that comes from and through perseverance. Persevering is simply insistence of yourself to endure through difficulties. It's the externalization of the interplay of your psychological toughness and the wealth of your knowledge.

In the cesspool of Trenton State Prison, I became acquainted with Gautama Buddha. His insights greatly impacted my outlook on and approach to life. I learned how to manage my feelings while in the moment, how past choices determine my future trajectory, and how to develop strategies for success. One of the best strategies I incorporated is to NOT waste time or opportunities. Once they're gone, they're not coming back. This strategy required me to hone my forward-thinking, discipline, and self-critiquing abilities. I had to work on and invest in myself. I learned that anything worthwhile only came with effort. Unlike some who probably had nothing or were given everything, I knew I had to work at obtaining the life I wanted. There's a popular saying by motivational speaker, Jim Rohn, which says (paraphrased): "If you work hard on your job you'll make a living, but if you work hard on yourself you'll make a fortune." This saying relentlessly sizzles in my mind now just as it did when I was in prison. Back then it helped prompt me to begin working on myself. A key practice for me was to question myself daily and untiringly. I found that working on myself was paramount to writing my own narrative - authoring my living story, in real-time, as it unfolds.

Know that there's faith needed when writing your living story. My personal growth and empowerment came from a reliance on both faith and facts. Life isn't all factual; it's emotional and irrational at times. So faith in oneself requires taking chances and trusting yourself in your abilities to achieve and to take risks. Serious self-questioning had me acquire this level of faith.

To discover what you think of yourself and learn some amazing things about yourself, routinely ask yourself:

- What kind of life do I desire for myself?

- How am I spending my time?
- Am I taking advantage of every good opportunity that comes my way?
- Am I making good decisions or are they countering my dreams of success?
- Do I engage in activities and entertain thoughts that are developing me or destroying me?
- Is my self-esteem where it needs to be and not where I want it to be?
- Is my inner strength and determination strong enough to resist difficult times?
- How will I respond to rejection or failure?
- Am I embracing challenges or cowering from them?
- Am I growing towards my best self?
- Am I a confident or doubtful decision maker?
- What are my fears? Am I ruled by them?
- Can I turn the negatives in my life into positives?
- Am I willing to take a chance on my abilities?
- Am I a complainer or am I solutions-oriented?
- Do I believe in myself?

- Do I take disciplined action to act on an idea when it appears or do I defer acting on it until a later time?
- Do I want to make a living or make a fortune in life?
- Do I neglect my dreams?
- Do I have a personality that attracts or repels people of success?
- Do I really love myself?
- Do I know my value?
- Do I know my triggers?
- Am I proud of where I am in my life?
- Am I living up to my full potential?
- Do I see any value in failure?
- Am I hopeless and nihilistic?
- Do I forgive myself?
- Do I forgive those who hurt me in the past?
- Am I anchored to the worst parts of my life?
- Can I let go of the pain from my past traumas?
- Who do I want to be? Do I believe I can become that person?
- Am I associating with people because they tell me what I *want* to hear or what I *need* to hear?

- Do I act on constructive criticism or disregard it?
- Do I commend myself when I do something well?
- Do I have good habits?
- Am I overly critical of myself?
- Do I overthink myself to failure?
- Am I a pessimist or an optimist?
- Am I a leader?
- Do I have the courage to act on my intuitions?
- Do I care more about what others think of me than what I think of myself?
- Am I willing to make the tough choices or do I go with the easier ones?
- Do I quit when things get hard or painful?
- Am I on the right path in life?
- Do I govern myself with integrity?
- Do I have something to contribute to the well-being of another?
- Can I become a source of hope and inspiration for others?
- Am I worthy of people investing their time, talent, faith, and resources in me?
- Do I spend enough time on myself?

- Do I want to be an owner or renter?
- Am I worthy of respect from others regardless of their title, position and wealth?
- Do I respect others regardless of their title, position and wealth?
- Is the quantity or quality of years of my life most important?
- How do I gauge what an accomplishment is?
- Am I willing to sacrifice now for later reward?
- How do I benefit from my knowledge and talents?
- What motivates me?
- Do I have a fight or flight mentality when things get hard?
- Am I the one who's writing the story and directing the movie of my life?
- Are my goals ambitious or mediocre?

The Gift of Wisdom

In the same vein that social revolutionaries, community activists and organizers seek redress to the problems of governmental abuse, injustice and inequality by first critically questioning the practices of social institutions, we must do the same on an individual level. We should critically question ourselves to redress the problems with our mindset. Our behavior reflects our thinking and our thinking reflects our mindset. A common phrase goes, “As you think, so shall you become.” I personally think I’m an amazing man. I didn’t merely survive a few harrowing, nightmarish ordeals. I defeated and overcame the government-funded racialized mass incarceration project created to steal my soul. Yes, I am amazing!

We’re each created with unique abilities. When we take authorship of our story and critically excavate the deep recesses of our psyche, then become introduced to ourselves through adversity, we then discover how incredible we really are. These amazing qualities may be exemplified in you being an amazing mother, father, sister, brother, musician, cook, artist, counselor, speaker, friend advisor, life coach, mentor, first responder or teacher. It is your story to write and reveal to yourself and the world.

My story exhibits the human capacity to transform despite adverse external pressures and circumstances. It embodies how the strength of the human spirit, the creative force of human imagination, and the power of love can empower the human will and determination to thrive in spite of its limitations.

I'm a modern day phoenix - discarded into the fiery hell of America's mass incarceration as a Black child and emerged from the ashes into an illumined, self-actualizing, amazing Black man. My success is my proof!

What I share here is my daily inner dialogue that allows me to sculpt, shape, and recondition my mindset. I offer to you a blueprint to do the same. Self-talk is a confidence boosting exercise that can shift every dimension of your life for the better. The motivational speaker Les Brown said, "Inner dialogue will determine the quality of your life." So go ahead -

talk with yourself and encourage yourself. Be the greatest salesperson of *you* that you know. It takes courage to believe in yourself then act on that belief. It's an incredible feat to accomplish.

As a kid I always enjoyed comic books. As a kid (and even now as an adult) I read graphic novels and watch superhero movies based on comic books. They showcase humanity in various forms, good and bad. They also provide social commentary and critique of present day human reality while exemplifying models of human exceptionalism. We all have a talent or gift that uniquely belongs to us. It's an ability that distinguishes us from others. These talents not only benefit us, they help others. Bryan Stevenson, lawyer and author of *Just Mercy,* successfully saved innocent men from being executed on death row and drastically impacted how juveniles are now sentenced in America's criminal justice system. Just as amazing is the unknown person who has a gift for being a nurturer and understanding how to care for children. They use this gift to own and operate daycare centers to provide early education opportunities for kids while supporting the needs of working parents. Each of our gifts are unique. We can't waste them and are responsible for using them to be our best self while bettering others along the way.

I have devoted the use of my gifts and amazingness to change the narrative of system-impacted people and returning citizens. My work, my calling, is to free as many of my brothers and sisters, my surrogate family, left behind in the dungeons of America's mass incarceration. A great number are needlessly languishing in prison as a result of racialized law enforcement practices and sentencing policies. I'm determined to be an advocate for them and help their voices get heard. With others we can change unjust systems and our economically devastated and disadvantaged communities. This change begins with first improving ourselves while possessing an immovable commitment to personal success.

Just Getting Started

As I conclude penning words for this volume, my story is still in the making. I am still in the act of becoming. Each day I'm a step closer to my fullest potential because I'm forever a student of life. I've already paid a debt for my childhood transgressions that took so much from me and others. Now I get to benefit from those hard times by contributing to life in a compelling and extraordinary way. The price and purpose of my journey's destination is non-refundable and non-negotiable! Counterproductive forces that rise up against my goals will find no space in my mind or heart. A laser-focused and solid work-ethic will help sustain me. No hand-outs or charity, or pity. I've never been about that life.

I'm now *doing* things and no longer just thinking and wishing about them. The fulfillment of my visions, dreams and goals are burned onto the walls of my mind. They're sewn into my mind's eye as if they were painted pictures. What I've desired to do with my life now resonates in my thoughts like beautiful, melodious echoes of a sweet song on mountaintops.

As part of my work, I've been mentoring justice-involved young boys and girls who are affected by opioid addiction. I go into detention facilities, schools and alternative program sites to share my story and offer my insights while listening to the challenges they're facing. My goal is always to be transformative in my interactions, never transactional. I've developed mentoring curriculum programs for reentry service organizations and have facilitated returning citizens support groups. I'm assisting lawyers and families to understand how the powerful social justice model of *Participatory Defense* can achieve a just outcome for people who have encountered legal cases against them. It's such a critically important work. The results save lives with every interaction.

Since I can't be everywhere to share my life lessons in person, this book is meant to share it for me. The process of textualizing my life's chronicles was a lesson in itself. It demanded that I get comfortable with the torrent of uncomfortable feelings and defiant impulses swelling inside me as I wrote about my vulnerabilities. The feelings summoned forth William Earnest Henley's poem, *Invictus*, because of the impact it has had on me. His 16-stanza work emphasizes the admirable goal of self-jurisdiction, and its last line recounts, "I am the captain of my soul." This helps me understand that the purpose of this book is greater than my discomfort. This journey forced me to grow even more into the very characteristics, qualities and mindset I encourage others to follow.

Writing was also a painfully difficult exercise but as the saying goes, "Nothing worthwhile should come easy for us." Strenuous achievements are a prerequisite for success in life. If you believe that progressing in life should not be a difficult, challenging or an uncomfortable experience, this book is not for you.

I desire that everyone find their inner hero or actualize their best self. I believe a hero reveals themselves only by ***first*** becoming themselves. Pain and adverse conditions are often the provocations needed to discover our heroic aspects. It doesn't require wealth, privilege, or a great physique. We need only to have a committed, fearless desire to triumph over anything.

Joseph Campbell, the author of *A Hero of a Thousand Faces*, shared that, “Heroes embody the best qualities in humans, but they almost always start out with nothing.... The quest forces the hero to use strength, wits, or both to defeat an enemy or some type of monster that crosses their path in hopes of preventing them from completing the quest.”

I believe I discovered the magic of transforming personal pain and suffering into beautiful poetics in my life. My greatest lesson I want to pay forward is: *To not run from but in the direction of life’s beautiful pain.* It’s a pain or ordeal in life that forges within you a strong resolve, a resolve that is averse to making excuses or settling for less than best efforts. It transforms pain and gives rise to an inner voice that cheers you on. This pain must be faced and it exists as an affirmation of your self-doubt or self-confidence and won’t recede until you begin to believe in yourself. Once you believe in yourself, your best self arrives for others to benefit from. Others treat you how you treat your own self.

In the classic Japanese literary work entitled *The Book of Five Rings*, its protagonist, Miyamoto Musashi, who was a samurai, wrote of a void that separated what the master and student knew. We should not fear testing the limits of what we know and are capable of doing simply because we don't know how it may turn out. The voids in our lives must be entered into because our successful becoming depends on it. I have audaciously entered it. I have arrived on the other side of it as the Master Designer of my success. Mastering something is the prelude to the ability to master many other things. Never settle for having just one talent or skill set. I encourage myself daily that I do not yet know everything I must know. This keeps me humbled and hungry for more success! So, in your successful becoming:

1. Never stop developing yourself!

2. Practice enjoying your accomplishments!

3. Create vision boards with goals you WILL achieve!

4. Make a bucket list of activities you WILL do!

5. Pursue mastery of your mind along with acquiring skill sets!

6. Interact with people transformatively and not solely transactionally!

A Beautiful Pain is my continuing journey. Pt II is on the horizon.

About The Author

Damon D. Venable is a Rutgers University School of Criminal Justice graduate with a degree in Finance and a New Jersey State Certificate in Paralegal Studies. He has over twenty-five years of paralegal experience. He is a Community Advocate and currently works as a Paralegal assisting in preparing resentencing hearings for children who were tried as adults and youth offenders under twenty-six years old. He coordinates with community members to develop defense strategies to secure favorable outcomes for these children and young adults.

He is a Reentry Preparation Consultant, Peer-to-Peer Mentor, and a Professional Development Coach. After being arrested at age sixteen for serious first-degree offenses, on May 4th, 2021, Damon was released on his earliest parole eligibility after serving thirty-five years of his life sentence. He remains a staunch proponent of the Restorative Justice model and endeavors to transform the Criminal Justice System from a structure that mistreats people of color.

www.ingramcontent.com/pod-product-compliance
Lightning Source LLC
Chambersburg PA
CBHW051825090426
42736CB00011B/1650

* 9 7 9 8 9 8 7 1 7 8 2 1 8 *

Appendix A: Peek into My Prayer Life

Over the years things come and go in my time with God. For over 20 years though, I have been praying this revised *Prayer of Jabez* daily *(1 Chronicles 4:10)*. I recommend creating or using a special prayer that you pray daily. It will be an anchor in a world of change.

My morning time with God starts with...

A prayer:

Lord, please bless me
Please bless me indeed
Please expand my territory
May your hand lead me and guide me
Please keep me from temptation,
so that I do not cause You or anyone else pain
Please fill me with Your joy, contentment, obedience,
power, love and peace
Please increase the size of my shield of faith, to deflect
the flaming arrows of the evil one
May I walk in courage, fearing no man
May I never doubt my call
Amen.

Spiritually dressing for the battle:

I then read and pray Ephesians 6:10-20a slowly. We are in a spiritual battle daily; this reminds me of that.

A Psalm of praise and promises:

I then slowly recite Psalm 145.

Praying for America and leadership in government:

As I put the American flag out by our front door.

Couch time:

Bible Reading, Journaling, Listening, and Praying... usually as I eat breakfast on the couch with a huge cup of coffee!

Appendix B: God's Love in Poetry

I do not consider myself a poet, but these thoughts and feelings came to me while finishing the book. God's merciful love has increasingly overwhelmed me these last few years.

<u>Savor of Heaven</u>

Soaking in love
Alone yet immersed
Brushing of arms with eternity
A tingle, a spark, a touch departed
Glimpse of radiance, glorious life
Treasures of heaven, intense glory that fills
Piercing warmth penetrates heart and soul
Eyes blink, eternity flashes, radiant light blazes
Royal heirs, myriads adorned in splendor
Fleeting brushes with glorious inheritance
Vapor fading, radiant warmth remains
Gift from the King, His treasures given
Savor of heaven

<u>The Ruby</u>

Glorious chamber
Once dim, coming alive
Light brightens; countless treasures radiant
Beaconing joy, love, fullness, life-filled
Space, a gap, centered for all to see
Glorious gift, on pedestal raised
Love aglow, a prize, overwhelming eyes
A jewel loaned, bequeathed to His beloved
Bursting with splendor, tasted, consumed
Enveloping and lifting, pouring and filling
Pure radiance, overflowing beauty
Red-filled ocean of love
The King's gift to me
The Ruby, my Wifey

www.ReadCraigCarter.com

www.ingramcontent.com/pod-product-compliance
Lightning Source LLC
Chambersburg PA
CBHW022008100426
42736CB00041B/1034
9798992341706